Access EAP

FOUNDATIONS

Course Book

Sue Argent
Olwyn Alexander

Garnet
EDUCATION

Published by
Garnet Publishing Ltd.
8 Southern Court
South Street
Reading RG1 4QS, UK

www.garneteducation.com

First published 2010

ISBN: 978 1 85964 524 6

British Cataloguing-in-Publication Data
A catalogue record for this book is available from the
British Library.

Production

Production manager: Pam Park
Project manager: Jo Caulkett
Project consultant: Rod Webb
Editorial team: Jo Caulkett, Sue Cope, Julie Moore
Design and layout: Mark Slader, Christin Helen Auth,
                          Mike Hinks
Illustration: Doug Nash
Photography: corbis.com, gettyimages.com,
                          istockphoto.com, fotosearch.com
Audio: Recorded at Motivation Sound
                          Studios, produced by EFS Television
                          Production Ltd.

Printed and bound in Lebanon by International Press:
interpress@int-press.com

The authors and publisher would like to thank the
following for permission to reproduce copyright material:
Definitions on pages 104 and 195 from Macmillan
Dictionary © Macmillan Publishers Limited 2010, reprinted
by permission of Macmillan Education.
Text and graph on pages 181–182 reproduced with kind
permission of John Cook, http://www.skepticalscience.com.
Temperature trends graph on page 182 reproduced by
permission of American Geophysical Union.
Website extract on page 20 reproduced with kind
permission of UCAS.
Text on page 185 reproduced with kind permission of the
Parliamentary Office of Science and Technology.
Text on page 193 printed with kind permission of the
Fairtrade Foundation (http://www.fairtrade.org.uk).
Extracts on pages 18 and 102 adapted with kind
permission of Cambridge University Press.

Author acknowledgement

We would like to thank all those who gave us valuable
feedback on early drafts of this book, in particular
the readers and editors at Garnet Education and our
colleagues, Jane Richardson, Tom Pritchard and George
Woolard. We are especially grateful to Jane and Tom
and their students for their intelligent and perceptive
suggestions when piloting the draft material as a course.

We would also like to thank the following for their
subject-specific expertise and advice: Professor Brian
Austin (School of Life Sciences, Heriot-Watt University)
on laboratory health and safety; Jennifer Argent on
Environmental Science Studies; Iain Argent on Computer
Science Studies. Any errors in the book are our fault and
result from not asking these people the right questions.

Finally, many thanks to family, friends and teaching
colleagues who gave us permission to present them in the
pages of this book as staff at Gateway University. You
know who you are.

Sue Argent and Olwyn Alexander, February 2010

Contents

	Unit themes	Functions	Texts	Academic language
1	Preparing for university studies	• stating purposes • meeting other students	• conversations with new students • university websites, letters and application forms • student personal statements	types of nouns word families collocations formal and informal style to + verb so that + sentence have to
2	Freshers' week	• describing position, shape and movement • contacting staff	• map • case study • e-mails • university website guidance notes	shape nouns noun phrases to name places prepositional phrases for position and movement there is / are
3	First steps and new routines	• instructions and processes • describing purpose, method, sequence, frequency and duration	• how to instructions • lecture on laboratory health and safety • lectures on linear and cyclical processes • flow diagrams	noun phrases to name steps and to show sequence articles starting sentences prepositional phrases for method and sequence general and specific vocabulary passive verbs
4	Finding information	• comparing • contrasting • evaluating advantages and disadvantages	• assignment question • student discussion • flier for library • library lecture • texts from Internet • sources for an assignment	general nouns to name features noun phrases to start sentences general to specific organization more than / less than positive and negative adjectives
5	New ideas and new concepts	• defining • classifying • analyzing • giving examples	• student diary • introductory lectures • definitions • student university assignment draft • student discussion • tree diagrams	general nouns to name classes general to specific ideas in sentences/tree diagrams synonyms prepositional phrases for specific information in definitions relative pronouns
6	Borrowing and using ideas	• describing change and development	• lecture • student discussion • extract from textbook • tutorial • student discussion • introductions to essays • timelines • spidergrams	general nouns to summarize starting sentences with topics transitive / intransitive verbs used to + but general to specific verb tenses
7	Something to say	• introducing self • contributing to discussions • giving a presentation	• committee meeting • minutes of a meeting • presentations • feedback discussions • student discussions	patterns to show interest, confirm and refine ideas word stress sentence stress
8	Linking ideas	• explaining reason and result / cause and effect • giving levels of probability	• short talk • quiz • flow diagrams • health information website • student high school essay draft • feedback discussion • student university assignment draft • tutorial discussion • model paragraphs	general nouns to summarize familiar ideas starting sentences with familiar ideas general to specific development in noun phrases patterns to show probability prepositional phrases for reasons and results result + because; reason + so; as a result + reason; reason + makes
9	Supporting ideas	• reporting data • comparing and contrasting • explaining trends • supporting claims with data • interpreting data	• annual report extract • marketing proposal • university league table • tables and graphs	noun phrases to label data general to specific organization to persuade patterns to show relationships in data patterns to show a viewpoint familiar and new ideas in data prepositional phrases for data: more than / most
10	Exams	• all functions	• student discussion • health information website • exam questions • extract from a textbook • tables and graphs • tutorial discussion • library lecture	review functional language review noun phrases language of exam questions

ACCESS EAP: Foundations

Writing and speaking	Academic competence	Thinking critically
· **Speaking**: name academic subjects; discuss purposes and expectations · **Writing**: write purpose statements; complete a form	· listen and read with a purpose · choose and record vocabulary · use dictionaries · support statements with specific information	• think of reasons why • identify student purposes • guess word meanings • compare English with your language • evaluate examples for relevance • evaluate expectations
· **Speaking / Writing**: describe position; describe a campus · **Speaking**: ask about names · **Writing**: study plans; feedback	· university's expectations of teachers and students · prepare to listen · take responsibility for learning · constructive feedback	• identify feelings • suggest an improvement • guess subject areas • evaluate e-mails • find specific examples
· **Speaking**: ask questions in a lecture; ask and answer questions about purpose and method. · **Writing /Speaking**: describe processes from instructions and flow diagrams	· predict organization and content of a lecture · ask questions in a lecture · make notes in flow diagrams · share listening and note taking · record and learn vocabulary	• identify text purposes • evaluate sentences • identify a problem
· **Speaking**: brainstorm ideas; exchange information; oral summaries · **Writing**: sentences to compare and contrast; the introduction to an assignment	· redraft ideas for a reader · use reading to support listening · lecture organization · make a checklist to evaluate sources	• identify advantages and disadvantages • support claims with reasons • identify viewpoint
· **Speaking**: numbers · **Speaking / Writing**: synonyms; reconstruct a text from tree diagram notes · **Writing**: definitions; classification systems; examples	· recognize quick explanations · analyze concepts · the Dewey Decimal system · organize, record and learn key vocabulary · take notes for a purpose	• predict pressures on students • evaluate definitions • evaluate synonyms in context • improve definitions • identify the purposes of examples • support explanation with examples
· **Speaking**: oral summaries · **Writing**: an e-mail; sentences to show changes; sentences from notes; the introduction to an assignment	· share listening focus · take notes on a timeline · organize vocabulary · analyze an essay question · borrow ideas correctly · work together in an acceptable way	• find information relevant to an audience • evaluate a student draft for acceptable borrowing
· **Speaking**: participate in a discussion; give a short presentation; use intonation and stress to show interest and confirmation and to focus listeners' attention · **Writing**: presentation checklist	· reasons why you have to contribute to discussions · recognize and respond to contributions · presentations · give feedback on speaking	• evaluate contributions in discussions and presentations
· **Speaking**: answer quiz questions · **Speaking / Writing**: give reasons for feedback; explain hazards; give feedback on writing · **Writing**: Redraft texts; explain causes and effects	· make notes in flow diagrams · analyze assignment tasks and titles · be aware of reader · use feedback to redraft assignments · EAP assessment criteria · refer to people in an academic way	• evaluate student texts • compare student texts with models • identify attitudes in student–lecturer interactions
· **Speaking**: discuss Internet access in your country · **Writing**: e-mail to a friend; report on Internet access in your country	· understand tables and graphs · support claims with objective data · use persuasive moves · use feedback to redraft a report	• identify viewpoint • select data to support claims • interpret data • evaluate claims using a checklist • evaluate a website
· **Speaking**: give a short talk and answer questions · **Writing**: take notes from a text to answer a question	· revise strategically for exams · classify and record functional vocabulary · use practice exams effectively · review exam results · set goals	• link general concepts to specific examples • identify relevant information • interpret data

Introduction

What is different about this book?

It's about university

Access EAP: Foundations is based on real student life and prepares you for many of the tasks that you will face while doing a degree at an English-speaking university. It shows what life is like at university by introducing three students at the beginning of the first semester at Gateway University in Summerford, somewhere in the UK. Each unit follows their progress as they have conversations and discussions, listen to lectures, read texts, work on assignments and make choices about how to study.

The themes

Each unit has a theme relating to the early weeks of study at a university and explores what the lecturers will expect from you at this stage in the academic year. You will develop the language you need to meet these expectations, for example, comparing ideas, explaining cause–effect relationships and interpreting data in tables and graphs, as well as writing assignments and e-mails and joining in discussions. We have adapted reading and listening texts that are really used at university, so that you can practise study strategies and develop vocabulary and grammar patterns that you can use when you start your academic studies.

The lessons

There are ten units in the book, with each unit divided into five lessons. The first lesson in each unit is quite easy and often introduces an aspect of Gateway University such as the campus map, the library, the history of the university or the students' union. We have linked the listening, reading, speaking and writing tasks together around each theme, just as they are at university. The three students have regular conversations to discuss aspects of their studies and how they feel about them, so that you can learn about what to expect when you are at university. There are also regular tasks in each lesson to develop your ability to think critically and to study effectively.

An important part of each lesson is the self study task, which often helps you to develop the vocabulary, grammar and skills introduced in the lesson. To help you to build up your vocabulary, there are lists of key words from the texts which are useful for academic study, and there are regular tasks to help you to understand, learn and practise these key words. You will learn the important grammar patterns that are needed for understanding and producing academic texts. This means that you will learn a lot about nouns and noun phrases rather than verbs. You will also learn how to write good texts by moving from general to specific and from what is familiar to what is new. These aspects of academic grammar are quite different from general English, but they are essential for understanding academic style.

Progress

Access EAP: Foundations is designed to help you to make progress, to achieve a higher level of language and study skills. The tasks and texts start with things that you know, but they become more challenging in the later lessons, leading to a practice exam at the end. However, you will meet the same key ideas and key language in different lessons, helping you to remember them as you work through the book.

Unit 1

Preparing for university studies

Lesson 1
Hello

Aims

- to meet the students in this book
- to prepare for meeting other students at university
- to understand the differences between purposes and expectations

Gateway University is in Summerford, in the UK. At the end of the long summer vacation, a number of students are already on the university's main campus, in order to prepare for the next year of studies. Some students come to university with clear purposes. Chen, Maysoun and Guy know why they are studying the degree subjects they have chosen. They have expectations about what it will be like to study here, but it is not possible to know everything. There will be a lot to learn this year.

Key words

the vacation
a number of ...
the campus
studies
purposes
degree subjects
expectations

Task 1 Listening

⊙CD1-1 **Listen to some students meeting for the first time, in the hall of residence[1] and in the campus supermarket. Complete the table below.**

name	country	course	degree subject	year or level
		English		
		English		

Chen

Task 2 Thinking critically

2.1 Who started the conversation and why?

2.2 Put the students in the table below according to age. Write your reasons.

	student	reason
oldest		
youngest		

Guy

Maysoun

[1] In some countries, this is called a *dormitory*.

We studied in the summer <u>to</u> learn English for university studies.

P

Chen   Maysoun

At university, students have to write much longer texts than they write at school.

Maysoun   Guy

I'm studying Computer Science so that I can get a good job with a high salary.

Chen

There isn't much writing in a Computer Science course.

Task 3 Pre-listening

Read what the students say on the left-hand side of this page and on page 9. Write P next to the purposes and E next to the expectations. The first one has been done for you.

Discussion
- What are your own purposes in studying at university?

Task 4 Listening

⊙CD1-2 Listen to this conversation in the coffee shop and complete the table below.

student	purposes	expectations

Task 5 Thinking critically

Which expectation in the table above will probably not be correct? Why?

Discussion
- What are your expectations: what will university study be like for you?

Task 6 Noticing language

6.1 Look again at the students' statements on this page and on page 9. Underline the words that show purpose. The first one has been done for you.

6.2 Study the key words from the conversations in Tasks 1 and 4 (see page 200). Notice how the words are used. Find five nouns, two verbs and three adjectives.

6.3 Find words in the conversations that often go together. Use them to complete sentences a–f. The first letter is given to help you.

We call these word partners *collocations*.

a Chen is studying Computer Science to get a job with a

h_____ salary.

b Guy is studying I_____ Business in order to get

a job where he can travel.

c Global climate change is an environmental

i_____.

d In the coffee shop, the students discussed their choice of

degree s_____.

e There are environmental issues in d_____

countries as well as developed countries.

f Maysoun wants to learn a_____ these issues.

I chose this course to learn about environmental issues in developing countries.

Maysoun

I think my course will involve a lot of reading.

Study smart

1 Write a list of subjects that students in your class want to study at university. Make sure you can write and say your subject correctly.

2 Working with other students, choose three words from the key word lists for this lesson. Check all of them in three different dictionaries, including an electronic translating dictionary and an English-only learner's dictionary.

Discuss which dictionary is best for:
• helping you to say the word correctly
• finding word families (noun, adjective, verb)
• finding useful collocations

I'm studying International Business in order to get a job where I can travel and meet interesting people.

Guy

There'll be students from lots of different countries on my course.

Task 7 Speaking

7.1 Listen again to the conversations from Tasks 1 and 4. In the transcripts on page 200, highlight the useful words and phrases for meeting new students.

7.2 Close your books and work in groups of three. Practise what to say when meeting new students.

Task 8 Writing

8.1 Look at the tables on pages 7 and 8. Write a sentence about each student.

8.2 Write similar sentences about your classmates and check each other's texts.

Self study

From the key words lists for this lesson, choose five words that you think will be useful to learn. Are they nouns, verbs or adjectives? Find and learn any of their collocations. Learning collocations will help you to use these words in your own writing.

Lesson 2
Language study

Aims
- to use key words from Lesson 1
- to understand and use language patterns for purpose statements
- to recognize and practise simple purpose statements

Task 1 Using key words correctly

1.1 Complete the word families for the useful key words below. Write the correct word forms in the empty spaces in the noun and verb columns in the table.

1.2 Choose a noun or a verb from the left-hand columns to complete the sentences column correctly. You may need to change the form of the word.

	noun	verb	sentences
a	discussion		The class _____ the reasons for speaking to other students at university. This _____ took about five minutes.
b	studies		Maysoun and Chen decided to _____ English for university _____.
c	expectation	.	Maysoun _____ to read a lot on her course. However, Chen's _____ that he will not have to write much on a Computer Science course is probably not correct.
d	choice		Maysoun went online to _____ a computer. She also discussed her _____ with Chen.
e		introduce	It is important to _____ yourself to other students at university. The first part of an essay is the _____.

Task 2 Matching

Match the beginnings and endings below to make purpose statements. Write the correct number in each box. The first one has been done for you.

a Students work hard in order to ☐ 2   **1** he can get a good job with a high salary.

b Maysoun and Chen studied in summer to ☐   **2** pass exams.

c Guy is studying International Business to ☐   **3** they can learn from each other.

d Students start conversations in order to ☐   **4** learn about environmental issues.

e Chen is studying Computer Science so that ☐   **5** learn English for university studies.

f Maysoun chose her course to ☐   **6** travel and meet people.

g Students often work in groups so that ☐   **7** get to know each other.

Noticing grammar patterns

Purpose statements

The grammar patterns below are often used for purpose statements.

pattern		example
in order to	+ verb	*in order to learn*
to		
so that	+ sentence	*so that he can get a good job with a high salary*

Task 3 Practising grammar patterns

3.1   Complete the sentences below. Use the grammar patterns from the box above.

a Chen and Maysoun studied in the summer _____ .

b Chen is studying Computer Science _____ .

c Maysoun chose her course _____ .

d Guy is studying International Business _____ .

e Students often work in groups _____ .

**3.2   Read the first part of one of the statements above to your partner. Ask '*Why?*'
Your partner should give a suitable answer using *to, in order to* or *so that*,
<u>without</u> looking at her/his book. Take turns to ask and answer.**

Task 4 Reading quickly to find information

The text below is from a page for international students on the Gateway University
website. Its purpose is to explain three important features of the university.

Read the text for *one minute only.* Tick ☑ the three features it explains.

university location ☐   help with study ☐   academic subjects ☐

sport and fitness ☐   social life ☐   computer facilities ☐   health ☐

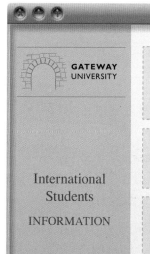

**GATEWAY
UNIVERSITY**

International
Students

INFORMATION

The lecturers put their lecture notes and coursework on
the intranet so that you can complete any missed work,
and they all have an appointment system so that you
can get help if needed.

The University Health Centre has an open day in the first
week of term to show students what to do and where to
go if they have health problems.

In Freshers' Week[2], the university organizes social
events so that students can get to know each other and
join university clubs. For example, the International
Club organizes trips and talks so that students can learn
about Summerford. Also, students can use the club's
noticeboard to advertise for language partners in order
to practise the languages they want to learn.

Key words

lecturers

the intranet

an appointment
system

the health centre

problems

organizes

social events

clubs

trips

the noticeboard

to advertise

partners

[2] At some universities, this is called *Orientation Week.*

Task 5 Reading carefully to understand details

Read the text from Task 4 again more carefully. Answer the questions below using purpose statements.

a Why does the university have a Freshers' Week?

_____.

b Why do some students advertise for language partners?

_____.

c What is the purpose of the Health Centre open day?

_____.

d What is the purpose of the lecturers' appointment system?

_____.

Task 6 Thinking critically

6.1 Chen is planning to go to a talk organized by the International Club. Why?

6.2 Guy is advertising on the noticeboard for a language partner from China. Why?

Task 7 Noticing grammar patterns

Underline the purposes in the text from Task 4. How many begin with *to* ( ), *in order to* ( ), and *so that* ( )? Write the correct numbers in the brackets.

Task 8 Noticing collocations

Cover the key words list on page 11. Find collocations in the web page text to complete the sentences below.

a You have to use the appointment _____ to see a lecturer.

b Gateway University has a Health Centre to help with health _____.

c Students go to _____ events in Freshers' Week to get to know each other.

d You have to _____ the languages that you want to learn.

Task 9 Speaking and writing

9.1 Read the text on page 11 again. Close the book and tell another student what you can remember.

9.2 Together, write to an English-speaking friend at another university, explaining how Gateway University supports international students.

> **Discussion**
> • What other support would you expect a university to provide for international students?

Self study

Find university websites and look for information for new students. Copy and paste the purpose statements into a document. Print them and bring them to the next class.

Lesson 3

Reading with a purpose

Aims
- to understand and practise different purposes for reading
- to contrast formal written expressions with informal spoken expressions
- to choose key words to learn and use correctly

Discussion
- How do you read a newspaper, a website, an e-mail or a timetable in your language? Which ones do you read quickly, slowly, carefully or several times? Do you do the same when you read in English?

Task 1 Before you read

Maysoun applied for her course in Environmental Studies before she left Syria. She received a letter from Gateway University.

How do you think she read this letter? Tick ✓ one of the boxes below.

a slowly and carefully, checking all the words she did not know in her dictionary ☐

b quickly, in order to find out if her application was successful ☐

Task 2 Reading quickly to find information

Look at Maysoun's letter below. Does she have a place at university? How do you know?

Mrs Maysoun Saleh
114, Althawrah Street
Damascus, Syria

GATEWAY UNIVERSITY

Dear Mrs Saleh
Confirmation of a place to study at Gateway University
This is to certify that the above-named has been offered and has accepted a place to study at this university.

Yours sincerely

Sandra Rose

Sandra Rose
Postgraduate Admissions Officer

Reference:	10074711
Qualification:	Master of Science (MSc) in Environmental Studies
Mode of study:	Full-time, on campus
Offer date:	23 June, 2009
Offer:	**Conditional offer**
Comments:	Please bring your degree certificate with you to registration. You are required to register on 17th September, 2009.
Start date:	18th September, 2009
Condition:	**Proof of ability in English language.** See the question and answer sheet for details of qualifications required.
Fees:	£10,450.00 You are required to pay your fees when you register.

Key words

confirmation
has been offered
has accepted
admissions officer
qualification
mode of study
conditional offer
registration
required
to register
condition
proof of ...
ability
fees

Postgraduate Office

GATEWAY UNIVERSITY

Questions and answers

Q What English qualifications do I need?
A If your first language is not English, you need to show that you would benefit from studying in English.

Acceptable qualifications
- You studied a first degree in English.
- You have a language qualification such as IELTS 6.5, iBTOEFL 90 or similar. Please ask the Postgraduate Admissions Officer about other acceptable qualifications.
- You studied on the pre-sessional course at Gateway University before your degree. A Grade C in the examination and a good report from your teachers would be sufficient proof of your English ability.

Key words

benefit from

acceptable

the examination

a report

sufficient

Task 3 Reading carefully to understand details

Look again at the letter on page 13 and the question and answer sheet above. Answer the questions below.

a Parts of the letter are printed in **bold**. Why?

b What does Maysoun have to do before she can start her degree?

c Who is the person she can ask for information about English language qualifications?

d When does she have to register for her degree studies?

e What does she have to do when she registers?

Task 4 Thinking critically

At the time she received this letter, did Maysoun have an acceptable level of English, as required? Give reasons for your answer.

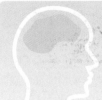

Study smart

Maysoun had a real purpose for reading her letter. She only checked her dictionary for words she needed in order to understand their meaning. She did not try to learn new vocabulary. When you read, try to read for a real purpose before you read again for a language learning purpose.

Noticing language

Stating requirements

The letter on page 13 is a formal letter telling Maysoun the requirements of the university.

Important letters use formal language, but there is usually an informal word with a similar meaning that we use when we speak.

Below are two ways to state requirements.

formal / written	informal / spoken
You are required to register on 17th September.	You have to register on 17th September.

Task 5 Practising language patterns

5.1   Find and underline the requirements in the letter on page 13. How would you tell a friend about these requirements?

5.2   Complete the table below. The first one has been done for you.

formal written expression	informal spoken expression
You are required to register on 17th September.	*You have to register on 17th September.*
You are required to pay your fees when you register.	
You are required to bring your degree certificate.	
You are required to have an acceptable level of English.	

Study smart

Find words that you did not know in the letter on page 13. Put them into two groups:

- words that you want to learn and use
- words that you needed in order to understand the letter, but that you don't need to learn now

words to learn and use	words needed only to understand the letter

Task 6 Using key words correctly

6.1 Complete the word families in the noun, verb and adjective columns in the table.

6.2 Choose a noun, a verb or an adjective to complete the example sentences. You may need to change the form of the word.

	noun	verb	adjective	example sentences
a		apply		Maysoun _____ for a place at Gateway University before she left Syria. Her _____ was read by the Admissions Officer.
b	success	succeed		Maysoun was _____ in gaining a university place, but in order to _____ at university, she needs to improve her level of English.
c		confirm		The Admissions Officer sent Maysoun a letter which _____ her place at Gateway University. This letter of _____ uses formal language.
d	condition			The letter gives Maysoun a _____ offer for a university place. The _____ requires her to show that she would benefit from studying in English.
e		accept		Maysoun _____ the offer of a place at Gateway University, but she decided to study on the pre-sessional course so that she could improve her English to an _____ level.
f			able	Maysoun has to get a Grade C in her language exam to prove her English _____ is acceptable.

Self study

Record and learn the word families for other words that you want to know. Write example sentences which contain the words you chose.

Lesson 4

Working on word meanings

Aims

- to follow formal instructions to complete an application form
- to identify different types of nouns and their meanings
- to use a dictionary to understand words with more than one meaning

When Maysoun chose to study at Gateway University, she applied for her course in Environmental Studies using an application form.

Task 1 Writing: completing a form

Complete the form below, using capital letters where required. Use the information from the letter on page 13. You do not have all the information you need, so you will have to make some guesses.

APPLICATION FOR POSTGRADUATE STUDY

Please return the completed form to:

The Postgraduate Admissions Office,

Gateway University, Summerford, UK

GATEWAY UNIVERSITY

Personal details of applicant

Family name (use capital letters): _____

Other names (use capital letters): _____

Title (circle as applicable): Dr   Mr   Ms   Mrs   Miss   Other: _____

Sex (circle as applicable): male   female

Marital status (circle as applicable): single   married   other

Date of birth: day _____   month _____   year _____

Country of birth: _____

Proposed study

Name of degree (use capital letters): _____

Type of degree (circle as applicable): by course   by research

Mode of study (circle as applicable): full time   part time   off campus/
distance learning

Entry date: _____ (courses on campus begin in September)

Proof of English ability (give details of English language qualifications):

_____

Key words

return ... to

the completed form

personal details

applicant

title

circle as applicable

proposed

type of degree

research

off campus

distance learning

Task 2 Thinking critically: making guesses

2.1 In Task 1, which information about Maysoun did you have to guess?

2.2 You probably did not know the meanings of some formal words in the application form. Which ones could you guess?

Task 3 Noticing language

The application form on page 17 contains forms of the word family *apply*.

3.1 Find and underline all the forms of *apply*. Write them in the word family table below.

verb	person noun	doing noun	idea noun	adjective
apply		applying		

There are three types of nouns in the table. They are used to name different things.

3.2 Complete the descriptions below.

a An _____ noun is used to name the whole process of applying for a university place and the documents this includes.

b A _____ noun is used to name a person who completes the form.

c A _____ noun is used to name the actions a person takes to apply for a university place, e.g., completing the form, sending the form to the postgraduate office, receiving an offer letter.

Task 4 Using key words correctly

English words often have more than one meaning. Below are parts of a dictionary entry for *apply*. There are three main meanings.

Choose the correct meaning for each sentence a–g. Write 1, 2 or 3 in each box. Then write the word class (noun, verb, etc.) used in each sentence. The first one has been done for you.

1
apply (verb)
request something, usually by writing or sending a form, e.g., *apply for a visa*
application (noun)
an official request for something

2
apply (verb)
relate to a situation or be important, e.g., *the rules apply*
applicable (adjective)
affecting or relating to a person or situation, e.g., *Circle as applicable: Ms/Miss/Mrs/Mr*

3
apply (verb)
use something for a practical purpose, e.g., *apply your knowledge to solve a problem*
applied (adjective)
used to describe a subject of study that has a practical purpose, e.g., *applied mathematics*

Cambridge Advanced Learner's Dictionary, 2008, Cambridge University Press

a China applied to join the World Trade Organization.   ☐ 1   <u>verb</u>

b Maysoun and Chen completed an application form
to study at Gateway University.   ☐   ____

c The requirements for entry to Gateway University apply
to all students.   ☐   ____

d Computer Science and Environmental Studies are applied
subjects.   ☐   ____

e Students who want to study in the UK have to apply
for a visa.   ☐   ____

f In some countries, age limits apply to people who want to
study there.   ☐   ____

g You can apply the skills you used to read Maysoun's letter
when you read other texts.   ☐   ____

Task 5 Thinking critically

**Try to find words in your language for the three different meanings of *apply* above.
Can you find one word for all three English meanings?**

You might need three different words. A word in English will not always have exactly
the same meanings as a word in your language.

Task 6 Noticing collocations

Find collocations in the application form on page 17 to complete the sentences.

a When you apply for a place at university, you are required to _____
an application form.

b The university needs your personal _____.

c Students can choose to study _____ campus or by _____ learning.

d You have to give details of your English language _____.

> ## Self study
>
> Choose some words that you want to learn. Make a word
> family for each word. Check the meanings in a good English
> learner's dictionary. Check if any members of the word
> family form collocations with other words. Try to write some
> sentences using different word classes.

Lesson 5

Explaining your purposes for studying

Aims

- to use guidance notes to evaluate personal statements
- to write purpose statements for university applications
- to give specific information to support purpose statements

When you apply to study at university, you have to complete an application form. You may also have to write a short text about yourself called a *personal statement.* This is included in the application, so that the university admissions team can get to know you as a person. They are particularly interested in the reasons why you have chosen the subject and the university, in other words, in your purposes. Your personal statement will be more convincing if you are clear about your purposes.

Key words

a personal statement

is included

particularly

reasons why ...

convincing

clear

Task 1 Writing

Think about why you want to study at university. Write three statements about your purposes.

Task 2 Reading

The guidance notes below are from a useful UK website (UCAS) that is designed to help students with their university applications.

Read the eight points below. Tick (✓) those that could be written using purpose statements, with the patterns you have learnt: *to, in order to* and *so that*.

Guidance notes

Below are some suggestions of points to include in your personal statement. These are for guidance only, so don't worry if some of the suggestions don't apply to you.

1 why you have chosen the course
2 evidence that you understand which skills and abilities are required to study the course
3 why you want to go to university to study
4 any other achievements that you are proud of, e.g., achieving Grade 3 piano or being selected to play for a local sports team
5 positions of responsibility that you hold / have held, both in and out of school, e.g., work for a local organization
6 how you want to use the knowledge and experience that you gain

If you are an international student, also give your answers to these questions:

7 Why do you want to study in this country?
8 What evidence do you have to show that you can successfully complete a university course that is taught in English?

Key words

suggestions

points

evidence

skills

achievements

being selected

hold positions of responsibility

a local organization

gain knowledge and experience

successfully

Task 3 Reading and thinking critically: purposes

Below are three draft personal statements by international students who are applying to different universities.

3.1 **Underline any purposes.**

3.2 **Next to each purpose, write the number of the relevant guidance notes from page 20.**

Student 1

> I love to travel and Canada is a very interesting country for study. I have always been fascinated by electronic engineering and I read a lot of books on this subject. I won first prize in my college engineering competition last year. This is my dream to solve problems and challenges. Your university is very famous with many experts. I believe that I should study to a high level so that my parents can be proud of my achievements.

Key words

fascinated
solve problems
challenges
experts

Student 2

> I have enjoyed studying and learning about electronic engineering for many years. I wish to study in New Zealand to give me a step forward and to gain the right skills needed to succeed academically and professionally. I am a hard-working person and always do my best. Your university is highly respected and I chose this degree course to show me the way to help my country and the industry in my country to develop.

Key words

academically
professionally
highly respected
industry

Student 3

> I decided to study in the UK to broaden my view of the world. Also to improve my English to give me a good position in an international company with high salaries. I chose Computer Science for a degree subject in order to use my mathematical skills fully and I have always been interested in it. I will use my degree to help my country develop as a global economy, and the friends I meet in the UK will help in this.

Key words

broaden my view
use ... fully
a global economy

Task 4 Reading and thinking critically: specific information

Here is another guidance note on writing personal statements.

> Give specific information to make the statement more convincing and more personal.

Find any *specific* information given by the students above. Which student gives the most specific information about purposes?

Task 5 Writing specific information to support purposes

Write the best specific example (1–7) to support each purpose statement (a–d) below.
Note that some of the examples are not very convincing, either because they are too general or because they are not relevant.

a I believe that I should study to a high level so that my parents can be proud of my achievements. For example, _____

_____

_____.

b I wish to study in New Zealand to gain the skills needed to succeed academically and professionally, especially _____

_____

_____.

c I decided to study in the UK to broaden my view of the world. For example,

_____

_____

_____.

d I chose Computer Science in order to use my mathematical skills fully, especially

_____

_____

_____.

1 I have very good grades in Maths

2 after graduating, I would like to do a specialist master's course

3 this is a very interesting country

4 at university I will meet people from other countries, and I can learn about their cultures

5 the ability to work in a team to solve problems

6 they want me to work hard

7 in programming and software design

Key words

specialist
cultures
in a team
programming
software design

Task 6 Writing and reviewing

6.1 Add specific examples to your three purpose statements from Task 1 to make them more personal and convincing.

6.2 Exchange with another student and read each other's texts. Say what you like about them.

Discussion

- Have your expectations of university study as an international student changed as a result of what you have read and discussed? If so, in what ways?

Self study

Find key words on pages 20 and 21 that you would like to use to explain your purposes for university study. Check the meanings in a good English learner's dictionary and add them to your text from Task 6.

Lesson 1
Finding your way around

Aims
- to understand the description of a location (a place)
- to listen to information in order to find locations on a map
- to learn language for describing locations

New students have to learn their way around the university to find key locations. Guy is a helper for new students. He is on duty in the central square on the main campus. He is outside the admin building handing out campus maps. He is surrounded by students and is trying to answer their questions.

Key words

locations
the central square
the main campus
outside
the admin building
maps
surrounded by ...

Study smart

Look at the map below. What is the number of the circle that shows Guy's position? You are going to listen to a conversation and identify the other locations on the map. To prepare, either study the map or read the conversation transcript on page 201.

Task 1 Listening

ⓐ **CD1-3 Listen to the conversation. Match each location below to a location on the map. Write the correct number in each box.**

a Electronic Engineering

b Geology

c Management and Accounting

d the nearest open-access computer laboratory

e Biology (Professor Watson)

f Amartya Sen Lecture Theatre

g Alan Turing Laboratories

h bus stop

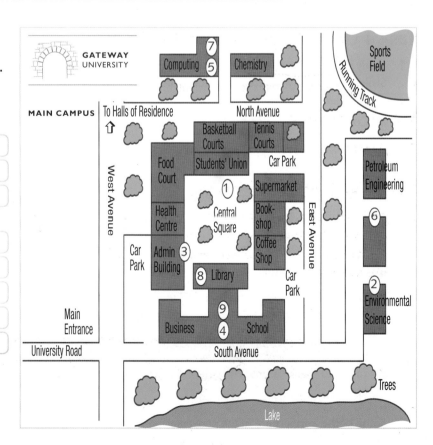

Study smart

Think about how you prepared to listen. Which helped most, studying the map or reading the conversation transcript? Why?

Task 2 Thinking critically

2.1   Why does Guy say "Wait! Wait!"? How do you think the new students are feeling?

2.2   Suggest a better way to organize the students so that they can explore the university.

Task 3 Noticing language

The key words below from the conversation in Task 1 have been sorted into two groups. Position words show *where* the location is. Campus locations are the *names* of places.

Choose at least five more words or phrases from the conversation to write in each column.

position words	campus locations
outside	the central square
in	the Business School

Task 4 Understanding position words

4.1   Study the descriptions of key campus locations below. Which of them are incorrect? Strike through any incorrect position words and write the correct position words above them.

   a   Computer Science is in the ~~south~~ *north* of the campus.

   b   Geology is behind Petroleum Engineering and Environmental Science.

   c   Guy is in front of the admin building.

   d   The Alan Turing Labs are in the east of the campus.

   e   Professor Watson's office is on the ground floor.

   f   From Guy's position, the library is on the left.

   g   Guy is in front of a line of students.

   h   The bus stop is behind the students' union.

   i   The library is behind the students' union.

   j   The Health Centre is behind the admin building and the food court.

   k   To get to the Amartya Sen Lecture Theatre, you have to walk round the library.

   l   The main entrance is on West Avenue.

4.2   Some of the answers are in the conversation from Task 1. Listen again and see if you were correct.

Noticing grammar patterns

Describing locations

To describe a location such as a university campus, the speaker or writer often uses *There is* (singular) or *There are* (plural), particularly to begin sentences.

Example: *There is a bookshop between the supermarket and the coffee shop.*

Task 5 Practising grammar patterns: writing

Complete the sentences below about the campus using the pattern from the box above.

a _____ trees in _____ of the Petroleum Engineering Building.

b _____ a car park _____ to the students' union.

c _____ a large food court _____ the central square.

d _____ a sports field in the _____ east of the campus.

e _____ open-access computer labs _____ most buildings.

f _____ halls of residence in the north _____ of the campus.

g _____ a Freshers' Week helper _____ the central square.

h _____ free shuttle buses _____ the Hydrology Workshop.

Task 6 Practising grammar patterns: speaking

6.1 Describe a location on the campus map for others to name, or name a location for others to describe.

6.2 Record a voice message to arrange to meet a friend somewhere on the campus.

Task 7 Writing

Work in pairs. Write sentences about your school building or campus using *there is/there are* and position words from this lesson.

Examples: *There are trees outside the classroom.*
The library is on the top floor.

Self study

Make a note of any words in the key word list for this lesson that you would like to use.

Find university websites with campus maps. Print one and bring it to class in order to practise describing key locations.

Gateway University has named some of its buildings after famous academics: Alan Turing, Amartya Sen and Rachel Carson. Find out which of our three students, Chen, Guy and Maysoun, might study their work, and explain why to other students at the next lesson. Find out about a famous academic in a field that you are interested in.

Lesson 2

Language study: shape, position and movement

Aims

- to recognize noun phrases
- to understand a set of key academic shape words
- to recognize and use shape, position and movement language

Gateway University is a large university with several campuses. It has many laboratories and lecture theatres. These academic buildings are given specific names in order to help students to find their way easily.

Noticing grammar patterns

Noun phrases for naming locations

In the listening task from Lesson 1, students wanted to know how to find:

- the Alan Turing Laboratories
- the Amartya Sen Lecture Theatre
- the nearest open-access computer laboratory

These names for buildings are all examples of noun phrases. We use nouns to name objects (*laboratories*), people (*students*) and ideas (*access*). When we need to be more specific, we can add nouns (*computer laboratories*) and adjectives (*new students*) to say which buildings, people or ideas we mean.

pattern	example
article + noun + noun	*the computer laboratories*
article + noun + noun	*the Alan Turing laboratories*
article + adjective + noun	*the open-access laboratories*

Noun phrases are groups of words that work together as nouns.

In academic texts, noun phrases are extremely important. They show academic ideas clearly because they name them specifically.

Task 1 Noticing grammar patterns: identifying noun phrases

Underline the noun phrases in the sentences below.

a The Geology Department is between Petroleum Engineering and Environmental Science.

b The Alan Turing Laboratories are on the top floor.

c The bus stop is in front of the students' union.

d The library is opposite the students' union.

e The Health Centre is between the admin building and the food court.

f To get to the Amartya Sen Lecture Theatre, you have to walk through the library.

g The main entrance is on West Avenue.

Task 2 Noticing grammar patterns: analyzing noun phrases

Label the noun phrases in the signs below. Write adj–n (adjective–noun) or n–n (noun–noun). The first one has been done for you.

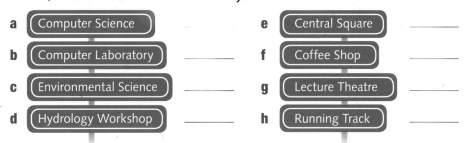

a Computer Science

b Computer Laboratory _____

c Environmental Science _____

d Hydrology Workshop _____

e Central Square _____

f Coffee Shop _____

g Lecture Theatre _____

h Running Track _____

The pictures below show what things look like (shape), where they are (position) and where they are going (movement). Most of the language for finding key locations is about position and movement.

This book is *next to* the lamp.

These students are going *into* the coffee shop.

A basketball is *round*.

Key words

shape
position
movement
key locations

Noticing grammar patterns

Prepositions with noun phrases

Prepositions, e.g., *behind* (position) and *through* (movement), are used with noun phrases.

pattern	example
preposition + noun phrase	*There is a car park behind the admin building.* *To get to the Amartya Sen Lecture Theatre, the students walk through the library.*

Task 3 Using prepositions correctly

3.1 Add a preposition from the box below to each noun phrase to complete the sentences. Use each preposition only once.

| towards | on | on | round | along | to | behind | opposite |

a Computing is _____ North Avenue.

b Every evening, Guy runs ten times _____ the running track.

c The library is _____ the students' union.

d The bus goes _____ South Avenue.

e The Alan Turing Laboratories are _____ the top floor.

f The students are walking _____ the main entrance.

g The Business School is _____ the library.

h The bus goes _____ the Hydrology Workshop.

3.2 Now put the prepositions in two lists, one for position and one for movement.

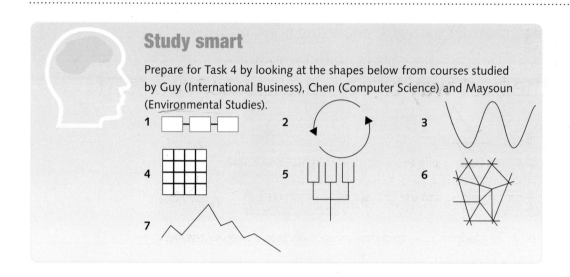

Study smart

Prepare for Task 4 by looking at the shapes below from courses studied by Guy (International Business), Chen (Computer Science) and Maysoun (Environmental Studies).

Task 4 Thinking critically

Study these noun phrases for shapes. Identify the academic subject that each noun phrase is most likely to belong to and give your reasons.

a	a sound wave		
b	a food chain		
c	a river network		
d	a planning grid		
e	wave power		
f	a supermarket chain		

g	a management network		
h	a tree diagram		
i	a water cycle		
j	a peak price		
k	chain code		
l	a family tree		

Key words

a wave

a chain

a cycle

power

a planning grid

a code

a tree

a network

peak

Task 5 Understanding noun phrases for shapes

Match each noun phrase a–l, above, to a diagram, 1–7, in the Study smart box. Write the correct number in each box. Underline each key shape word in a–l.

Task 6 Writing

Write about your school or campus. Write short answers to the questions below using some of the words and phrases you have learnt in this lesson.

Example: *Describe the position of the nearest shopping mall.*

It is in the west of the city, near the river.

1 Where is the library? _____

2 Where is the nearest bus stop? _____

3 Where does the bus go? _____

4 Describe the position of the nearest car park. _____

5 Describe the position of the nearest sports field. _____

6 Where can students buy books? _____

7 How do you get to your teacher's office? _____

8 How do you get to the student canteen? _____

Self study

Choose a topic that interests you and find a text about it in a book or on the Internet. Make a note of useful shape, position and movement words. Bring them to share at the next class.

Lesson 3

Finding the best way to communicate with staff

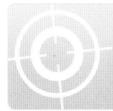

Aims
- to use a case study to learn about communicating with university staff[1]
- to understand and use names and titles correctly

During Freshers' Week, many students have to communicate with their university teachers for the first time.

Discussion
- How do you and your teachers communicate outside class time? How do you expect to communicate with your new teachers at university? Do you think it will be easy, or could there be problems?

Case studies are long examples used in university teaching to help students to understand ideas. They are also designed to make students use critical thinking to apply these new ideas to real life.

A case study

Maysoun is in the library open-access computer lab. She has finished writing e-mails to her father in Syria and to her husband, who is visiting his PhD supervisor[2] in London. She clicks on the university website and goes to the noticeboard for Environmental Science postgraduates. She wants to find out about next week's activities. After reading the notices, Maysoun realizes that she has to communicate with her tutor, Dr Charles, for the first time. She has not yet met Dr Charles. She decides that it's best to send an e-mail.

Task 1 Reading headings

Look at the e-mails on pages 30–31. Name the writer of each e-mail.

E-mail 1

_____

E-mail 2

_____

E-mail 3

_____

E-mail 4

_____

---

[1] Professors, lecturers, tutors (in the UK system) or faculty (in the US system) and admin staff.
[2] *Advisor* in the US system.

Task 2 Reading quickly for the main idea

2.1 **What is the communication in the e-mails below about?**

2.2 **Write 1–4 in each box so the summaries are in the correct order.**

a Maysoun wants a meeting with Dr Charles. ☐

b Dr Charles tells Maysoun to choose a time. ☐

c Maysoun says she can't come on Monday at 9.15. ☐

d Dr Charles thanks Maysoun for letting her know. ☐

Task 3 Reading carefully for details

Look at the e-mails again. Give short answers to the questions below.

a How did Maysoun find out about the meeting?

b Maysoun has to take her son to school on Monday. Why is this a problem?

c What is Dr Charles going to leave for Maysoun at reception?

d How is Maysoun going to find her way around the department building?

e How can Maysoun find out when to meet Dr Charles?

E-mail 1

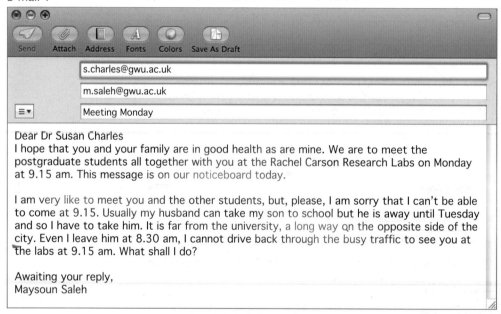

Key words

traffic

Send | Attach | Address | Fonts | Colors | Save As Draft

s.charles@gwu.ac.uk

m.saleh@gwu.ac.uk

Meeting Monday

Dear Dr Susan Charles
I hope that you and your family are in good health as are mine. We are to meet the postgraduate students all together with you at the Rachel Carson Research Labs on Monday at 9.15 am. This message is on our noticeboard today.

I am very like to meet you and the other students, but, please, I am sorry that I can't be able to come at 9.15. Usually my husband can take my son to school but he is away until Tuesday and so I have to take him. It is far from the university, a long way on the opposite side of the city. Even I leave him at 8.30 am, I cannot drive back through the busy traffic to see you at the labs at 9.15 am. What shall I do?

Awaiting your reply,
Maysoun Saleh

E-mail 2

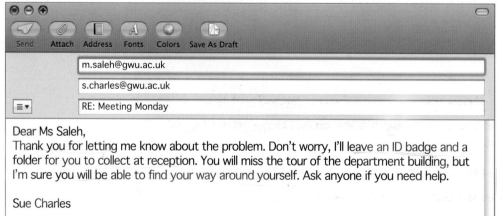

Key words

letting me know about

an ID badge

a folder

reception

the tour

Send | Attach | Address | Fonts | Colors | Save As Draft

m.saleh@gwu.ac.uk

s.charles@gwu.ac.uk

RE: Meeting Monday

Dear Ms Saleh,
Thank you for letting me know about the problem. Don't worry, I'll leave an ID badge and a folder for you to collect at reception. You will miss the tour of the department building, but I'm sure you will be able to find your way around yourself. Ask anyone if you need help.

Sue Charles

E-mail 3

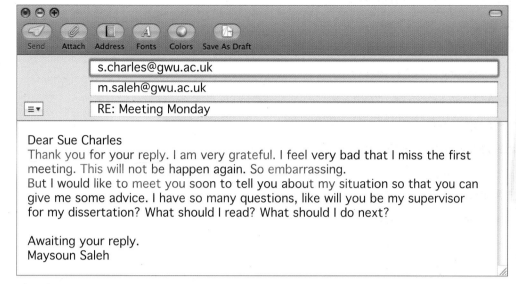

Key words

reply
grateful
embarrassing
situation
some advice
dissertation

To: s.charles@gwu.ac.uk
From: m.saleh@gwu.ac.uk
RE: Meeting Monday

Dear Sue Charles
Thank you for your reply. I am very grateful. I feel very bad that I miss the first meeting. This will not be happen again. So embarrassing.
But I would like to meet you soon to tell you about my situation so that you can give me some advice. I have so many questions, like will you be my supervisor for my dissertation? What should I read? What should I do next?

Awaiting your reply.
Maysoun Saleh

E-mail 4

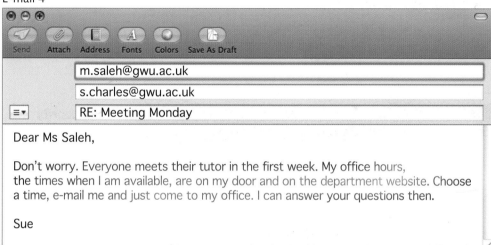

Key words

office hours

To: m.saleh@gwu.ac.uk
From: s.charles@gwu.ac.uk
RE: Meeting Monday

Dear Ms Saleh,

Don't worry. Everyone meets their tutor in the first week. My office hours, the times when I am available, are on my door and on the department website. Choose a time, e-mail me and just come to my office. I can answer your questions then.

Sue

Task 4 Thinking critically

Look at the e-mails again and answer the questions below.

a How does Maysoun find important information about her studies?

b Was e-mailing the best way for Maysoun to communicate with Dr Charles in this situation?

c Was the e-mail communication effective?

d Who wrote the longest e-mails? Why?

e How does Maysoun feel about missing the meeting?

f From Maysoun's last e-mail, what other feelings do you think she has?

g What can you say about Dr Charles from her e-mails?

Task 5 Noticing language for formal and informal style

Notice the language that is used in the e-mails and answer the questions below.

a What are the main differences between Dr Charles's e-mails and Maysoun's e-mails?

b Both writers change slightly in the way they open or close their e-mails. Find these changes.

c What are the differences between the case study e-mails and the English e-mails you write to friends?

When writing or speaking to people professionally, e.g., at university, it is important to get their names right. Usually, Western (English) names have two parts. The given names come first. There can be one or more. For example, one of the writers of this book is called *Olwyn*. These are the names that parents choose.

Last comes the family name, which is (usually) the same name as the father's family, e.g., *Alexander*. Be careful: some names can be either a given name or a family name. For example, in *Prince Charles* and *Charles Darwin*, *Charles* is a given name, but in *Dr Susan Charles*, it is a family name. English speakers often get confused by this and have to check.

Formally, you also have to know the title that a person uses. In the application for postgraduate study on page 17, there is a list of possible titles. To begin a formal written communication, the title followed by the family name is used, e.g., *Dear Ms Alexander*. With friends, people use the first given name without a title. When you know a teacher well, they may want you to be less formal with them and ask you to use their given name: *Please call me Olwyn.*

Task 6 Noticing language in names

In the left-hand column of the table below, circle the family names, underline given names and highlight titles.

Task 7 Using language in names correctly

Complete the table to show how to use formal and informal names.

full name	formal communication	informal communication
Dr Susan Elizabeth Charles		
Ms Caroline West		
Prof Robert Morris		
Dr Naseem Malik		

Most English-speaking universities have an international mix of students and staff. This means that many staff members do not have names based on the system outlined above. It is important to check a person's name by looking at how they write it, or by asking someone to say or spell it.

Example: *I'm sorry, I'm not sure how to write/say her/his/your name.*

Task 8: Speaking

Ask another student how to say or write her/his name.

Self study

Find a department staff list on an English-speaking university website. Choose some names and show how you would begin an e-mail to each member of staff. Bring what you write to share with the class.

Write a real e-mail to your teacher. Choose one of the purposes below.
- to arrange a meeting to discuss feedback on a draft
- to explain why you missed a lesson
- to offer to help with a visit to your university by some local schoolchildren
- to ask a question about something the teacher said in a lesson

Lesson 4

Finding the best way to study at university

Aims
- to understand how universities expect students to study
- to understand and give constructive feedback

Teaching staff in academic departments understand that studying at university is very different from studying at school, and that studying at an international university can be different from studying at your local university.

Task 1 Thinking critically

Think about your expectations about university. Have any of them changed?

Discussion
- What do you expect from teachers at university, and what do you think teachers at university expect from you? Make two lists.

There are many websites giving advice about what to expect and how to study effectively. While searching the Gateway University website, Chen found some guidance notes from his department, Computing and Electronic Engineering.

Task 2 Reading quickly for organization

Look at the guidance notes on page 34. How is the information organized? Tick ✓ the best answer below.

a two short paragraphs: one about teaching staff and one about students ☐

b two numbered lists: one about what students should do and one about what students should not do ☐

c two numbered lists: one about what teachers should do and one about what students should do ☐

d two numbered lists: one about academic work and one about school work ☐

Task 3 Reading carefully for understanding

Compare what the guidance notes on page 34 say with your own ideas about teacher and student expectations from the Discussion task above.

Task 4 Reading carefully to understand the text

Match the key words a–c, d–h and i–n below to their meanings as they are used in the guidance notes below. Write the correct number 1–3, 4–8 or 9–14 in each box.

a up to date ⬜   **1** final dates

b prompt ⬜   **2** modern, not out of date

c deadlines ⬜   **3** quick, on time

d challenging ⬜   **4** useful, helpful

e accurate ⬜   **5** able to meet

f with respect ⬜   **6** interesting, but makes you think and work hard

g constructive ⬜   **7** politely

h available ⬜   **8** correct

i a professional ⬜   **9** join in actively, e.g., ask questions

j a field ⬜   **10** hand in work for feedback or assessment

k feedback ⬜   **11** a subject area or area of study, e.g., Computing

l participate ⬜   **12** information about what is good and not good, e.g., what could be improved

m take responsibility ⬜   **13** a person in a job that requires good qualifications and skills, e.g., an engineer

n submit ⬜   **14** act independently, do things for yourself

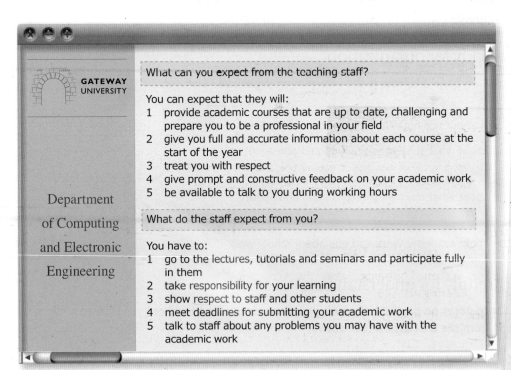

GATEWAY UNIVERSITY

Department of Computing and Electronic Engineering

What can you expect from the teaching staff?

You can expect that they will:
1. provide academic courses that are up to date, challenging and prepare you to be a professional in your field
2. give you full and accurate information about each course at the start of the year
3. treat you with respect
4. give prompt and constructive feedback on your academic work
5. be available to talk to you during working hours

What do the staff expect from you?

You have to:
1. go to the lectures, tutorials and seminars and participate fully in them
2. take responsibility for your learning
3. show respect to staff and other students
4. meet deadlines for submitting your academic work
5. talk to staff about any problems you may have with the academic work

Key words

up to date
challenging
professional
field
accurate/information
with/respect
prompt
constructive
feedback
be available
lectures
tutorials
seminars
participate in
take responsibility for
show respect to
meet deadlines
submit work

Task 5 Thinking critically

Chen is not sure that he fully understands the guidance notes for students on page 34. He would like a few examples.

Find specific examples of each of the notes on what students should do. Write a number 1–5 in each box. Sometimes, an example is relevant to more than one of the notes.

a e.g., tell your tutor if you are ill and cannot finish some work you have to do.

b e.g., carefully read any feedback comments from the lecturer on your work and try to apply them to the next piece of work.

c e.g., be patient with other students if you can't understand their English very well.

d e.g., don't be afraid to ask questions about things you haven't understood and answer questions when you can.

e e.g., start working on assignments early so that you can get feedback and finish the work by the due date.

Study smart

Work together with another student to add more examples to the ones from Task 5. Underline any examples in the list that apply particularly to you, i.e., that you feel you should do more.

Task 6 Noticing language patterns: collocations

6.1 **Complete the verb–noun collocations below from the guidance notes on page 34.**

a _____ responsibility for   **c** _____ deadlines

b _____ respect to

6.2 **Complete the adjective–noun collocations below from the guidance notes.**

a accurate _____   **b** constructive _____

Discussion

- What is the purpose of feedback on your writing, and who gives it? What kind of information would you find useful for feedback? Make a list.

Task 7 Reading quickly to identify purpose

On page 36 is some more information about expectations from the Department of Computing and Electronic Engineering website.

Read the text quickly and tick ✓ its main purpose from the list below.

a to introduce study skills   **c** to give advice to lecturers

b to explain a concept   **d** to give advice to students

Discussion

- Compare your expectations about feedback from the last Discussion task with the explanation in the text on page 36.

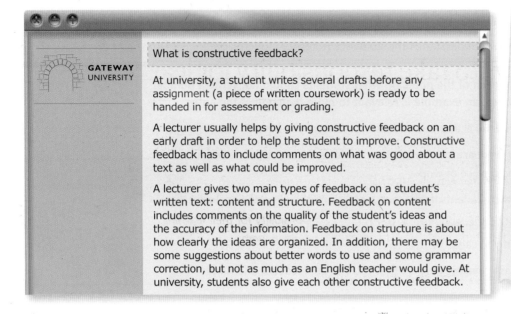

Key words

drafts
assignment
a piece of coursework
assessment
grading
to improve
content
structure
the quality of
the accuracy of

What is constructive feedback?

At university, a student writes several drafts before any assignment (a piece of written coursework) is ready to be handed in for assessment or grading.

A lecturer usually helps by giving constructive feedback on an early draft in order to help the student to improve. Constructive feedback has to include comments on what was good about a text as well as what could be improved.

A lecturer gives two main types of feedback on a student's written text: content and structure. Feedback on content includes comments on the quality of the student's ideas and the accuracy of the information. Feedback on structure is about how clearly the ideas are organized. In addition, there may be some suggestions about better words to use and some grammar correction, but not as much as an English teacher would give. At university, students also give each other constructive feedback.

Task 8 Thinking critically

Chen has written an e-mail to his former English teacher at his old high school. Because the teacher, John, is very friendly, Chen wrote an informal e-mail to tell him about life as a student at Gateway University. Chen has asked Guy to check the e-mail and give him feedback.

8.1 Read the e-mail below. Write notes on some constructive feedback for Chen. Comment on at least one good thing and at least one thing that could be improved.

8.2 This is an informal e-mail to a friend. Is there anything that would be incorrect in a formal e-mail to a teacher that Chen had not yet met?

Key words

reply
grateful
embarrassing
situation
advice
dissertation

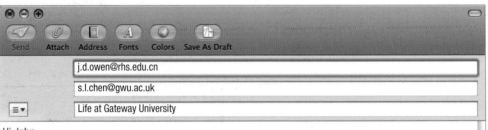

j.d.owen@rhs.edu.cn

s.l.chen@gwu.ac.uk

Life at Gateway University

Hi John,

How are you? I hope you have a good class of students this year, like me and my friends. I hope you remember us all! You asked me to keep in touch and tell you how I like UK, so here is my report!

I am OK. The campus is beautiful with lots of trees and a lake with ducks – very tasty! No, we don't eat them ☺ but we feed them sometimes. I live on the main campus in a big hall of residence. The other students are good. I am language partner for a guy called Guy (Ha Ha! Really that is his name!). He is learning Chinese, like you. But he is not so good as you yet. He also helps me a lot with my English. Everything is convenient. It has a sports field with a running track on the north west, so I can run every day to keep fit. It has computer labs in most buildings for everyone to use. Now I am e-mailing you at Petroleum Engineering, because it is outside the running track where I just ran. No problems yet except shopping and eating. Shopping is expensive. It has a supermarket on campus but the cost is a little bit high. With some friends we bought 5 kilo of rice in the Chinese supermarket at the city centre. We can share to make it cheaper. The canteen – called food court – is not bad prices but I miss my Chinese food. I am trying to cook some things for myself, like rice with tomato and egg, but I am a bad cooker. I start my real computing classes next week. Last week my EAP teacher said 'I hope you remember everything I told you because this is your very last English class, for ever!' What a shock, but maybe she is right. There is too much work to do in computing. I have seen all the lectures and labs and assignments for Semester 1 on our web noticeboard. No time for English class. ☺ I hope I will be OK.

John, I miss your jokes. Send me some!
From your hard-working ex-student.
Chen

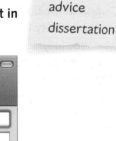

Self study

Find some guidance notes on a university website on how to study effectively at university. Choose about half a page of text and find words from the key word lists in this lesson. Make a note of the words that you think will be useful.

Lesson 5

Finding ways to take responsibility for learning

Aims
- to understand how students can take responsibility for their study
- to write personal study plan statements
- to review ways to study smart

In their EAP class, Maysoun and Chen learnt about taking responsibility for their learning.
Below is an extract from the study guidelines that their teacher gave them.

Task 1 Reading quickly for the main idea

Tick ✓ the best description of the EAP study guidelines below.

This text:

a gives a list of things students should do at university.

b describes students who study smart.

c gives a list of things teachers should do at university.

EAP guidance notes
Taking responsibility for your own learning is the most effective way to study. This is
what we call studying smart. Students who study smart do three things:
1. They are active and not passive: they do things for themselves.
2. They are not afraid to leave their comfort zone: they try new things and are not
   afraid of making mistakes; they don't just choose the easy tasks and familiar ways
   of learning.
3. They think about how they learn: they don't just complete tasks without thinking.

Key words
effective
active
passive
comfort zone
familiar

Task 2 Reading carefully and thinking critically

Below are some examples of how students study smart.
**Write the correct number in each box to show how the examples relate to the points in
the text above. Sometimes an example relates to more than one point.**

a They look for information.

b They try new ways of doing things and don't worry if they get things
wrong sometimes.

c They learn from their mistakes.

d They evaluate their learning.

e They don't get everything from the textbook or the teacher.

f They talk about their ideas in class.

g They ask questions in class.

h They ask themselves questions about what they are doing.

Task 1 Reading for writer's purpose

Texts 1 and 2 both give the same information. However, the texts have different purposes.

Answer the questions below.

a Which text tells the reader *what* to do? (This text gives instructions.)

b Which text tells the reader *how* something is done? (This text describes a process.)

c Which type of function – instructions or process – did you use to answer this question?

Task 2 Noticing grammar patterns

Look at Texts 1 and 2 again and answer the questions below.

a Find and circle three purpose statements in Text 1 and three in Text 2.

b Underline the noun phrases in each text.

c What are the differences in language patterns between the instructions text (1) and the process text (2)?

Noticing grammar patterns

Sentence patterns

Simple sentences in English have two parts: a starting point and a comment to say something new. In an instructions text and a process text, the sentences have a different starting point, so the way the sentences are organized is different. The verb form is also different.

	instructions	process
example sentence	*Heat* + *the solution.*	*The solution* + *is heated.*
sentence starting point	a verb	a noun phrase (names something)
sentence pattern	verb + noun phrase	noun phrase + verb
verb form	active *heat*	passive *is heated*

Task 3 Thinking critically

Look at the noun phrases + verbs below. Tick ☑ the real sentences. Cross ☒ the sentences which are not real. Change them into real sentences where necessary.

a The sand and salt mixture is put.

b The water is evaporated.

c The salt is dissolved.

d The mixture is poured.

e The sand and the salt are separated.

Noticing grammar patterns

Verbs with prepositional phrases

Some verbs, like *put* and *pour*, need something to complete them. You can use prepositional phrases (preposition + noun phrase) to describe position and movement, e.g., *on the top floor* and *round the running track*. In processes and instructions, a prepositional phrase can complete verbs like *put* and *pour* with this essential information, e.g., *The sand and salt mixture is put into water.*

Task 4 Practising grammar patterns

Cover the process text (2) on page 39 and say or write it using the instructions text (1) to help you. Start each sentence with a noun phrase.

Task 5 Thinking critically: process or instructions

Question:

A book can be supported a few inches above a table using a sheet of paper and an elastic band. How?

Answer:

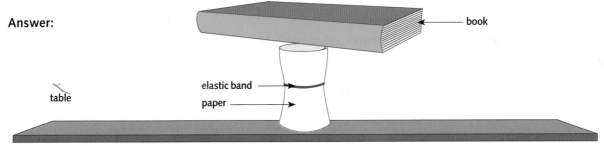

The table below contains a mixture of two texts giving the same information. They both answer the question above correctly. One is instructions and one is a process.

5.1 Write P (for process) or I (for instructions) next to each sentence.

5.2 Show the sequence (the order in time) of the steps by writing the numbers 1–4 in the table for each text.

	steps	process (P) or instructions (I)	sequence (1–4)
a	The cylinder is stood on a table.		
b	Secure the cylinder with an elastic band.		
c	The sheet of paper is rolled into a cylinder.		
d	Place the book carefully on top of the cylinder.		
e	The book is placed carefully on top of the cylinder.		
f	Stand the cylinder on a table.		
g	Roll the sheet of paper into a cylinder.		
h	The cylinder is secured with an elastic band.		

Key words

the cylinder
an elastic band
secure

Noticing grammar patterns

Articles in noun phrases

A noun phrase names something, e.g., *a book, the sheet of paper*. Writers use the indefinite article (*a* or *an*) and the definite article (*the*) in noun phrases to help the reader to understand what exactly is being named. The indefinite article (*a* or *an*) is for general naming, so *a book* means *any book*. The definite article (*the*) is for specific naming, so *the book* means *the book in front of us* or *the book in the previous sentence*.

Task 6 Noticing grammar patterns: articles in noun phrases

Text 3

How to support a book on a sheet of paper

Roll the sheet of paper into a cylinder.
Secure the cylinder with an elastic band.
Stand the cylinder on a table.
Place the book carefully on top of the cylinder.

Text 4

How a book is supported on a sheet of paper

The sheet of paper is rolled into a cylinder.
The cylinder is secured with an elastic band.
The cylinder is stood on a table.
The book is placed carefully on top of the cylinder.

6.1 Look at Texts 3 and 4, above. Is there any difference between instructions (Text 3) and process (Text 4) in the way that the writer uses articles?

6.2 How many definite and how many indefinite articles are used in each text?

Noticing grammar patterns

Articles for general and specific meaning
In instructions and processes, the first time something is named, it has a general (indefinite) meaning. When it is named again, later in the text, it has a specific (definite) meaning.

| general meaning (= *any*) | a / an + noun | *How a book is supported on a sheet of paper* |
| specific meaning (= *this*) | the | *The book is placed carefully on top of the cylinder.* |

Task 7 Practising grammar patterns: writing

Cover Texts 3 and 4. Complete the text below with the missing articles.

How (a)_____ book is supported on (b)_____ sheet of paper

(c)_____ sheet of paper is rolled into (d)_____ cylinder. (e)_____ cylinder is secured with (f)_____ elastic band. (g)_____ cylinder is stood on (h)_____ table. (i)_____ book is placed carefully on top of (j)_____ cylinder.

Task 8 Practising grammar patterns: speaking

Cover the process text (4) and say or write it. Use the instructions text (3) to help you.

Task 9 Writing and speaking

Close your book. Answer the two questions on pages 39 and 41 from memory. Use process or instructions; write or speak. Ask another student to check your answers.

Self study

Find English instructions on cans, food packets, medicines or the Internet. Write down any purpose statements in them. Find definite (*the*) and indefinite (*a/an*) articles.

Find some instructions in your own language and translate the purpose statements into English. Check that the articles follow the pattern you studied in this lesson.

Lesson 2

Beans on toast

Aims
- to make notes on instructions and processes in flow diagrams
- to understand and use language patterns for method and time in instructions and processes
- to understand and use language patterns for naming steps in processes

Chen is worried about spending too much money, so instead of their lunchtime language practice, Guy is teaching Chen how to cook an economical lunch that is very popular with students.

Task 1 Listening

CD1-5 Listen to the conversation. Make notes on the instructions by completing the steps in the flow diagram. One has been done for you.

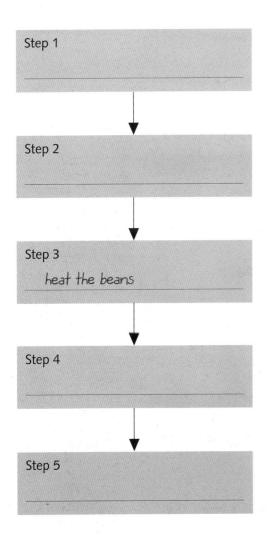

Step 1

Step 2

Step 3
heat the beans

Step 4

Step 5

Instructions for making beans on toast

First, open the can with a can opener and put the beans in a pan. Next, turn on the gas and heat the beans gently. Stir them with a spoon occasionally so that they don't burn at the bottom. Put two pieces of bread in the toaster and switch it on. Heat the beans until they just begin to bubble. Put the toast on plates and put the beans on top of the toast.

Task 2 Noticing language for purpose, method and time

Instructions often include information about purpose, method and time, as shown in the table below.

In the instructions for making beans on toast, find examples of each type of information and write them in the table. One has been done for you.

type of information	example
purpose – why?	
method – how?	*gently;*
time – when? (in what sequence)	
time – how often? (frequency)	
time – for how long? (duration)	

Noticing grammar patterns

Language for describing method

To explain *how* something is done, adverbs or prepositional phrases can be used.

language	pattern	example
adverb	adjective + *ly*	*carefully*
prepositional phrase	preposition + noun phrase	*with an elastic band*

Task 3 Noticing grammar patterns for method

In the instructions for making beans on toast above, find two adverbs and two prepositional phrases that show how something is done. Write them in the table below.

pattern	examples
adverbs: adjective + *ly*	
prepositional phrases: preposition + noun phrase	

Task 4 Practising grammar patterns for method

4.1 Answer the questions below using an adverb or a prepositional phrase. Work in pairs to ask and answer. Write the answers below.

a How do you open a can?

_____

b How do you stir something in a pan?

_____

c How do you connect a computer to the Internet?

_____

d How do you put out a fire?

_____

e How do you get to the Hydrology Workshop?

_____

4.2 Work with another student. Ask and answer a few more questions about method.

Processes

A process is a set of steps to produce or change something. There are thousands of manufacturing processes, for example, processes to produce cars, clothes and cans of beans.

Discussion

- Brainstorm the steps needed to produce a can of beans, from a farm to a supermarket. Compare your process with other students. Did you miss out any steps?

Task 5 Reading to understand sequence

The sentences below show the steps needed to produce a can of beans, but they are not in the correct sequence.

Show the correct sequence by writing the numbers 1–8 in the boxes.

a The cooked beans are poured into cans while they are still hot.

b The beans are removed from the bean plants by machine.

c Here, they are washed with clean water.

d Then they are transported to a factory by truck.

e Finally, they are transported to a supermarket by truck.

f Next, they are cooked together with the tomatoes and all the other ingredients until they are soft.

g The filled cans are sealed immediately and cooled for several minutes with cold water.

h The cold cans are labelled and packed.

Key words

- are removed
- the plants
- are transported
- a factory
- the ingredients
- soft
- are sealed
- immediately
- are cooled
- are labelled
- are packed

Task 6 Noticing language for sequence

6.1 Underline any words that helped you to understand the sequence of the steps in Task 5.

6.2 Three language patterns are used in the text to show sequence: signpost words, linking words and adjectives in adj–noun noun phrases.

Write examples from Task 5 in the table below. One has been done for you.

pattern	examples
signpost words at the beginning of sentences (four)	
linking words (one)	while,
adjectives in adjective–noun noun phrases at the beginning of sentences (three)	

Task 7 Practising language for sequence

Look at the process for canning beans, below, with the steps in the correct sequence. Complete the gaps with suitable adjectives to show the sequence clearly.

The beans are removed from the bean plants by machine. Then they are transported to a factory by truck. Here, they are washed with clean water. Next, they are cooked together with the tomatoes and all the other ingredients until they are soft. The (a)_____ beans are poured into cans while they are still hot. The (b)_____ cans are sealed immediately and cooled for several minutes with cold water. The (c)_____ cans are labelled and packed. Finally, they are transported to a supermarket by truck.

Task 8 Noticing language for method and duration

Find examples of language patterns for method and duration in the process for canning beans from Task 7. Write them in the table below.

type of information	examples
method – how?	
duration – for how long?	

Noticing grammar patterns

Nouns in flow diagrams
Textbooks often summarize a process using a flow diagram, to show all the steps in sequence.

The steps are usually labelled with the noun for each action (not the verb). To label the steps or stages in a process, it is important to understand how nouns and verbs are related in word families. All verbs have a _doing noun_ ending in -ing, e.g., **Living** in the countryside is healthy. Many also have an _idea noun_, e.g., **Life** in the countryside is healthy.

Task 9 Understanding word families

Complete the table below with nouns to match the verbs.

verb	doing noun	idea noun
a remove		
b transport		
c wash		X
d add		
e cook		X
f pour		X
g fill		X
h seal		X
i label		X
j pack		X

Noticing grammar patterns

Language for naming steps

Academic writers use idea nouns more frequently than doing nouns. When an idea noun (*removal*) is used in the noun phrases for steps, it is linked to the thing noun (*beans*) by a preposition (*removal of beans*).

Task 10 Using key language

Complete the flow diagram below showing how beans are canned. Use idea nouns to label the steps, or doing nouns where there is no idea noun.

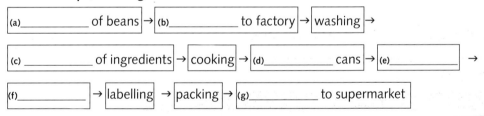

(a)_____ of beans → (b)_____ to factory → washing →

(c)_____ of ingredients → cooking → (d)_____ cans → (e)_____ →

(f)_____ → labelling → packing → (g)_____ to supermarket

Task 11 Writing

11.1 Write the process for canning beans from memory, using the completed flow diagram from Task 10 to help you. Remember to use some adjective–noun noun phrases to show the sequence of steps.

11.2 Check each other's work for the correct use of articles (*a/an, the*).

Self study

Find descriptions of processes in school textbooks. Write down any language for method, sequence, frequency and duration you find in them. Write down any idea nouns and doing nouns for labelling steps.

Lesson 3
Health and safety

Aims

- to understand language for purpose and method in a lecture
- to understand language for time (sequence, frequency, duration)
- to practise shared listening, note taking and asking questions in a lecture

Maysoun is having her first practical class in the Rachel Carson Teaching Laboratories. The topic is Health and Safety. Science laboratories can be dangerous places, and it is important that students and staff know how to stay safe when working in them. Professor Leach is going to begin the class by giving a short lecture.

Task 1 Preparing by predicting

Professor Leach has several aims for his introduction.
Predict the order in which you think Professor Leach will meet his aims by writing the numbers 1–4 in the central column of the table.

	aim	predicted order	actual order
a	make a joke		
b	introduce himself		
c	greet and welcome the students		
d	give an outline of the practical class		

Task 2 Listening for organization

⊙CD1-6 **Listen to Part 1, the introduction to the lecture, to check your predictions from Task 1. Write the actual order in the right-hand column of the table above.**

Discussion

- How does predicting help you to prepare for a lecture?

Task 3 Preparing to listen

Before listening to Part 2 of the talk, complete the exercises below.

a Discuss the possible dangers in a science lab.

b Work in pairs. Make a list of health and safety instructions for a science lab.

c Read the transcripts of Parts 2 and 3 of the talk if you wish, but don't change your lists. The transcripts are on pages 203 and 204.

Discussion

- In a lecture, is it better to make notes carefully or to listen carefully? Why?

Task 4 Shared listening for specific information

4.1 ⊕CD1-7 **Listen to Part 2 of the talk in pairs.**

Student A: On your shared list, tick the safety instructions that Prof Leach gives and make notes on any new ones.

Student B: Listen carefully but don't make notes.

4.2 ⊕CD1-8 **Change roles. Listen to Part 3 of the talk in pairs.**

Student B: On your shared list, tick the safety instructions that Prof Leach gives and make notes on any new ones.

Student A: Listen carefully but don't make notes.

Study smart

1 Work with your partner to review your list from Task 4. How many of your points were included in the lecture?
2 Work together with another pair of students to add more points from the lecture.

Task 5 Thinking critically

Can you think of any important points that Prof Leach missed? Give reasons why they are important.

Discussion

- What are the advantages and disadvantages of sharing listening with another student?

Noticing grammar patterns

Asking questions

In lectures, students often ask questions in two parts. First, they give the general topic (they say which part of the lecture the question is about). Then they ask the specific question.

Make your questions clearer and easier to answer by dividing them into two parts: general topic and specific question. Two useful patterns are:

You mentioned + noun phrase + specific question

You said + sentence + specific question

Task 6 Speaking

Use the table below to produce the students' two-part questions from the lecture on health and safety. Try to do this without looking at the transcript. Then look at the transcript on pages 203 and 204 to check your answers.

student	general topic	specific question
Maysoun	fire escape routes	How do we find these?
Angela	disinfectant	Where is it kept?
Peter	an experiment	Do we have to write a report?

Lesson 4

Processes in academic subjects: cycles

Aims

- to practise taking notes from lectures on cycles
- to share lecture notes to improve them
- to learn language for naming stages in cycles

Processes are important in academic subjects for describing how systems work. These may be natural systems, such as ecosystems and life cycles, or systems designed by humans, such as computer systems and management cycles, but they all involve processes. Processes from different subject areas all share the same features.

- They describe steps or stages in a sequence.
- They explain why, how and when things are done (using purpose, method and time language patterns).
- They can be summarized in flow diagrams, using idea nouns or doing nouns to label the stages.

Key words

systems

natural

share features

Task 1 Preparing to listen

Maysoun is at the first lecture in her optional module, 'Hydrology'. In this part of the lecture, Dr Charles briefly describes the water cycle.

Predict what Dr Charles is going to say. Draw a diagram to show the water cycle. What labels (names) will the stages have?

Task 2 Listening for information

CD1-9 **Listen to the lecture and change your diagram if necessary. Label your diagram correctly.**

Study smart

After listening, share your notes with other students and work together to improve them.

Discussion

- Is it a good idea to share notes in this way?

Chen is listening to the first lecture in his course, 'Introduction to management'[1]. In this part of the lecture, Dr Quinn briefly describes the P.I.E. cycle.

Study smart

The first sentence you will hear in the lecture is: *The P.I.E. cycle is a process for continually improving plans in an organization such as a business.* Can you guess what the letters P, I and E stand for? What shape will your lecture notes have?

Task 3 Listening and making notes

⊕ CD1-10 **Listen to the lecture and make notes on the P.I.E. cycle.**

Study smart

After listening, share your notes with other students and work together to improve them.

Task 4 Using key words correctly

4.1 **Complete the word families in the table below by writing an idea noun for each verb.**

4.2 **Choose nouns and verbs from the table and change them as needed to complete the sentences correctly.**

	verb	idea noun	sentences
a	improve		There are several processes designed to _____ plans continually in an organization. Continual _____ in any organization has to involve all staff.
b	specify		Some objectives are easy to _____; others are more difficult. There are different _____ for different systems.
c	implement		The second stage of the process is _____. If the plans are not _____, there will be no improvement.
d	evaluate		The results of any changes need to be _____. Every management process needs this _____ stage.
e	analyze		The results are carefully _____. This kind of _____ shows how effective the process is.

Self study

Find another cycle in a textbook or on the Internet. How many stages are there? Write the names of the stages.

[1] Introductory management courses are compulsory in a wide range of degree subjects.

Lesson 5

Processes in academic subjects: a design process

Aims
- to practise team listening and note taking in a lecture
- to develop awareness of academic vocabulary across subjects
- to take responsibility for learning vocabulary

Chen's first Computing Science lecture is an introduction to software development. Chen has to take notes on a process for designing software.

Task 1 Preparing to listen

Look at the flow diagram below. The lecture is about the waterfall model of software development. Why is the term *waterfall* used?

Task 2 Listening for specific information

⊛CD1-11 **Listen to the first part of the lecture. Circle the step on the flow diagram below that Dr Bell says is particularly important.**

The waterfall model of software development

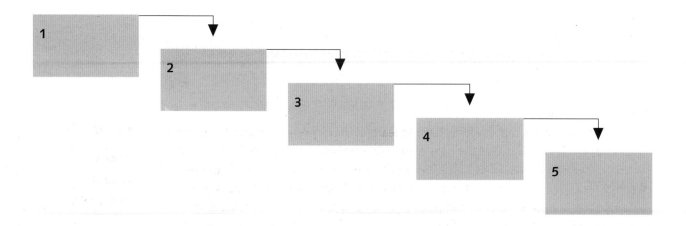

Task 3 Team listening for detail

⊛CD1-12 **Listen to the rest of the lecture. In groups of three, listen for different information.**
Student A: Write the five stages below in the correct order in the table.

| verification | design | implementation | maintenance | requirements analysis |

Student B: Listen for information about methods. Complete the methods column in the table.
Student C: Listen for information about purposes. Complete the purposes column in the table.

stages	methods: How?	purposes: Why?
a 1. _____	by _____ to people; carefully; in great _____	to make sure requirements _____
b 2. _____	by _____ what the software _____	so that _____ can be developed _____
c 3. _____		to make _____ efficient, adaptable and _____
d 4. _____	e.g., by _____ compatibility with other systems used by customers	to ensure that it _____ and is _____ to users
e 5. _____	e.g., by _____ problems; by _____ parts of the system	

Study smart

1 Work together to share your information and complete your tables.
2 Compare your notes with another team of three students.

Discussion

- What are the advantages and disadvantages of team listening?

Academic vocabulary

Some of the key words that students have to learn at university are technical or subject-specific terms. This means that they are used in one subject area and not in others, or have one meaning in one subject area and a different meaning in another. Examples of subject-specific vocabulary in Chen's lecture are *code* and *bug-free*. *Code* is used in Computing Science to refer to computer programs. It has a different meaning in International Business (e.g., *code of practice*) and Environmental Science (e.g., *genetic code*). In Environmental Science, *bug-free* also means something quite different. Lecturers in your subject areas will explain your subject-specific vocabulary.

Students also have to learn a lot of general academic vocabulary, for example, words such as *stage*, *analysis* and *evaluated*. These words are used in many different subjects, i.e., they are transferable. Lecturers in your subject will not explain these words, because you are expected to know them already.

Discussion

- How do you learn new words? Do you write them somewhere? What information about the new words do you note at the same time? Does this help you to use the words correctly?

Task 4 Noticing key language

Look at the key words below. Decide which are subject-specific vocabulary (S) and which are general academic vocabulary (G). Some words can be in both lists (B). Write S, G or B in each box.

technical ⬚   condenses ⬚   specific ⬚   runoff ⬚

cycle ⬚   programmers ⬚   evaporated ⬚   compatibility ⬚

hydrologic ⬚   system ⬚   precipitation ⬚

implementation ⬚   verification ⬚   objectives ⬚

Task 5 Learning words and important information about them

Below is an extract from Chen's vocabulary notebook. He wrote it after the lecture on software development. He checked in his dictionaries for some of the information.

5.1   How are the words in Chen's notebook organized? Tick ✓ the correct answer.

a by topic ⬚   **c** by date ⬚

b alphabetically, like a dictionary ⬚   **d** by grammar ⬚

5.2   Draw arrows to show what kind of information Chen noted. One has been done.

how to say the word
(word stress)

grammar details

an example of how it is used

grammar details

an example of how it is used

word family

how to say the word
(word stress)

grammar details

an example of how it
is used

word family

Semester 1 week 1
data (n. pl. ??? ask Guy) 数据 information / facts or numbers
Computers work on data very fast. If the data is wrong, the
results are wrong. (Guy said: GIGO = garbage in: garbage out!)
database, data stream, binary data

bug (n. sing.) 计算机病毒 a mistake in a program stops the
program doing what it should do.
In the first practical there was a bug in my program!
debug (v), bug free (adj)

verification (n. uncount.) 检查
checking stage to see if software works / can be accepted
by customer.
testing / evaluation
verify (v) verifiable / verified (adj)
In the verification stage, we have to make sure the program
works with the customer's other software.

meaning in Chen's
language

meaning in English

collocations

meaning in Chen's
language

meaning in English

meaning in Chen's
language

meaning in English

synonyms
(similar words)

Task 6 Thinking critically

In the first section of his notebook, for the word *data*, Chen wrote 'n. pl.??? ask Guy'. Why? What do you think was the problem?

Self study

Choose 15 words from this unit that are important for you. Record information about them, e.g., how to say them, their word families and their collocations. Write at least one example sentence for each. Ask a friend to test you on them. Then find two subject-specific words from your subject area. Prepare to explain their meaning to other students.

Lesson 1

Brainstorming and organizing ideas

Aims
- to find ideas for an assignment by brainstorming
- to use a table to organize information
- to understand and use language patterns to compare

Chen, Maysoun and Guy meet for coffee in Week 3 of the new semester at Gateway University. Already, they have coursework assignments to complete for some of their modules. Chen has a deadline for his first assignment in two weeks, so Maysoun and Guy decide to help him think about it. The question for his assignment is:
What are the advantages and disadvantages of computer-based learning compared with classroom learning?

Discussion
- Do you prefer to be in a classroom with other students or to use a computer to study?
- What kinds of things did you talk about? Compare your ideas with the words from the list in Task 1, below.

Task 1 Listening for the main idea

Chen, Maysoun and Guy brainstorm some ideas together.

⊙ CD1-13 **Listen to their conversation and answer the questions below.**

a Who prefers computer-based learning and who prefers a classroom?

b What kinds of things do the students talk about? Put a tick ✓ next to the ideas below that you hear.

cost

time

location

social group

convenience

fluency

flexibility

Task 6 Noticing language: positive and negative adjectives

Decide whether the adjectives in the box are positive or negative for learning. Write each one in the correct column of the table below. Two have been done for you.

| cheap | expensive | convenient | noisy | flexible | crowded | confident | sociable |
| reliable | efficient | accurate | rude | fluent | passive | effective | shy |

positive adjectives	negative adjectives
convenient	expensive

Task 7 Practising grammar patterns

Choose adjectives from the table above to complete the sentences below. Use the word in brackets to help you decide which adjective and which comparative form to choose.

a Computer-based learning is _____ than classroom learning.
   (advantage)

b Classroom learning is _____ than computer-based learning.
   (disadvantage)

c Classroom learning is _____ than computer-based learning.
   (advantage)

d Computer-based learning is _____ than classroom learning.
   (advantage)

Task 8 Thinking critically

Decide if each of the sentences below shows an advantage (A) or a disadvantage (D) of computer-based learning. Write A or D in each box.

a A shy student can be less passive on a computer than in a classroom. ☐

b You have time to be more accurate in computer-based learning. ☐

c You can learn to be more confident in a classroom. ☐

Task 9 Writing: supporting claims with reasons

When you say that one item is better than another, you make a claim, i.e., you give your opinion. Another person could disagree with you. In order to make your claim more persuasive, you can give a reason for your opinion.

Example:

Computer–based learning is more convenient than classroom learning, because you can study any time and you can take more time if you need to.

Think of some reasons to support the claims from Task 7. Write sentences like the one above.

Self study

Choose a topic that students in your class have different opinions about. For example, is it better to travel to classes by bus, car or bicycle? Write some comparisons to show which means of transport you prefer. Use positive or negative adjectives to show your viewpoint, and justify your opinion by giving reasons.

Lesson 2
Information sources

Aims

- to listen to a lecture which contrasts information sources
- to make a checklist to use to decide if sources are reliable
- to understand and use language patterns to contrast

Chen needs to go to the library to find more information for his assignment. He decides to go to one of the workshops run by the librarians at the start of each academic year to help students to use the library. Maysoun and Guy go with him.

In his first year, Guy was a little afraid of the library, because it seemed a very large and busy place. He mostly used the Internet to find information for assignments, but his lecturers want him to use more reliable sources.

Discussion

- Read the flier below advertising the library workshops. Can you answer *yes* to the questions?
- Look at the aims of the workshop. What do you think the lecture will explain? Compare your ideas with another student.

Get into the Library

GATEWAY
UNIVERSITY

- Do you know how to use the library?
- Can you locate the books you need for your assignments?
- Do you know how to find reliable information on the Internet?

Come to one of our workshops. We can help you to use the library and Internet effectively and efficiently.

Aims
We will:
- explain how sources of information are organized
- compare different sources of information to see which ones are more reliable

Workshops last about 45 minutes.

Key words

locate
workshops
effectively
efficiently

Task 1 Preparing to listen

1.1 Read the first part of the transcript for the library workshop lecture. Can you add more specific details to your discussion about what the library workshop lecture will explain? Will the lecture follow the order of the aims in the flier?

Part 1

Welcome to Gateway University library. My name's Marie Macdonald. Today, I'm going to give you a general introduction to the library so that you can learn to use it effectively and efficiently.

In order to use the library effectively, you have to be able to find reliable information from many different sources. You also have to know that the information is relevant for your purpose. In order to use the library efficiently, you have to be able to find relevant and reliable information quickly so that you do not waste your time. I'm going to cover two main aspects today.

- I'll start by contrasting the different sources of information and explain how you can decide which ones are more reliable.
- Then I'll explain how we organize the books and journals in the library so you can find them easily.

1.2 Decide if you want to read the complete transcript, on pages 206 and 207, before or while you listen.

Task 2 Listening for the main idea

ⓅCD1-14&15 Listen to the lecture. Which two items does Marie Macdonald talk about in this part of her lecture? Does she aim to show how these items are similar, or how they are different?

Task 3 Listening for detail

You used a table to take notes from the lecture, but you did not catch all the information.

3.1 Listen again and try to complete your table (Student A: see page 199, Table 1; Student B: see page 199, Table 2). Cover the other table while you work.

3.2 Work with a partner who has used a different table. Ask your partner questions to find the missing information in your table. Make sure you tell your partner the topic of your question before you ask the question. Use the features in the first column of the table to help you.

Example:

The librarian mentioned purposes of information. Why is information put on the Internet?

Noticing language patterns

Language for organization

The librarian introduced each part of her lecture by stating her main purpose and then mentioning the feature that she was going to use to contrast the Internet and the library. At the end of this part of the talk, she summarized the features to give a checklist, with some questions to use in order to decide if information is reliable.

Here are some of the signposts she used:

Let's think about the differences between …
First, we can think about purpose …
Then we can consider the viewpoint …
Another important difference … is the author.
So, to summarize what I've said …

Task 4 Understanding the organization of lectures

4.1   How did the librarian organize the lecture? Tick ✓ the correct pattern below.

   a She described the Internet and the library separately and listed all their features. ⬜

   b She took each feature in turn and contrasted the Internet and the library on the basis of just that feature. ⬜

4.2   Which features did the librarian use to show how the Internet and the library are different?

Task 5 Thinking critically

The librarian compared the Internet and the library in order to show that the library was a more reliable source of information. **Answer the questions below.**

a Do you think the librarian gave a balanced view?

b Did she consider different viewpoints?

c Does she admit in her lecture that there is another viewpoint?

d Can you think of reasons why the Internet is sometimes a good source of information?

Noticing grammar patterns

Contrasting ideas

There are three main ways to show contrast between sentences.

1 Use a linking word.
2 Use the same pattern in both sentences.
3 Use a signpost word.

1 Two sentences can be joined together using linking words such as *whereas* or *but*.

pattern	example
sentence + *whereas* + sentence	*People put information on the Internet in order to sell things, <u>whereas</u> we keep information in the library to build knowledge.*
sentence + *but* + sentence	*There are many web pages that sell goods and services, <u>but</u> there are others that sell ideas.*

2 The contrast is clearer if both sentences have the same pattern.

People put	information	on the Internet	in order to	sell things.
We keep		in the library		build knowledge.

There are	many	web pages	that sell	goods and services.
	other			ideas.

3 The sentences may not be linked, but there is a signpost word at the start of the second sentence to point the way to the contrast.

Example:

Anyone can publish their ideas on the Internet. <u>However,</u> published books and journals are usually written by experts.

Task 6 Practising grammar patterns for contrasting ideas

It is important not to confuse linking words and signpost words. Linking words can join sentences together, but signpost words can only point the way to the idea in the second sentence.
Below are some sentences which contrast ideas.

6.1 **Join each pair of sentences together to show the contrast clearly. Use a linking word or a signpost word.**

a Chen wants a good job with a high salary. Guy wants a job with opportunities to travel.

_____

b Maysoun expects her course will involve writing long texts. Chen expects his course will not involve much writing.

_____

c Chen likes white bread. Guy likes wholemeal bread.

_____

d Guy feels more comfortable learning in a classroom. Chen prefers learning with a computer.

_____

e Last year, Guy used the Internet to find information. This year, he is going to use the library.

_____

f Internet sources may have only one viewpoint. Library sources have a range of viewpoints.

_____

g Anyone can publish information on the Internet. Experts publish information in books and journals.

_____

h No one checks the quality of Internet sources. Experts check the quality of library sources.

_____

6.2 **Write two examples of your own to contrast ideas.**

Study smart

In her lecture, the librarian gave a checklist of questions. Use this checklist to evaluate information sources you find.

Purpose: Why has the information been published?
Is it trying to sell ideas?
Viewpoint: Does it show many different views?
Or does it show just one view?
Author: Is the author an expert in his or her subject?
Has he or she published a lot of other books?
Quality: Has the information been checked by other experts?

Self study

Find some information on the Internet about computer-based learning and classroom learning. Bring it to class to share with other students. Work in pairs or groups. Use the checklist from the Study smart box, left, to evaluate the information and the web page where you found it. Which features in the checklist are easy to find, and which are more difficult?

Lesson 3
Evaluating information sources

Aims
- to apply a checklist in order to evaluate information sources
- to analyze differences in style between different sources
- to recognize different types of noun phrases

Chen has found four sources on the Internet which seemed to be relevant to his assignment.

Discussion
- What information can Chen use to show where these sources are located on the Internet?

Internet locations are specified by a url, which shows the identity of the computer where the Internet page is stored. Urls can sometimes tell you about the person, company or organization who put the information on the Internet. Below are the urls for the sources that Chen found.

1   ◄ ► +   http://scholar.lib.gateway.edu/ejournals/LTEC/v25n4/Liu.html   ↻

2   ◄ ► +   http://www.classroomonline.com/   ↻

3   ◄ ► +   http://scholar.lib.gateway.edu/ejournals/LTEC/v30n2/Wu.html   ↻

4   ◄ ► +   http://roses4tea.blogspot.com/   ↻

Task 1 Thinking critically

1.1   **Who put the sources above on the Internet and why did they put them there? Choose from the list below. Use some words in the urls to help you. Write the numbers 1–4 in the correct boxes below. Give reasons for your answers.**

    a an organization, to help teachers to develop professionally ☐

    b an academic journal, to publish research in teaching ☐

    c an online bookshop, to sell books ☐

    d an individual person, to tell their own stories ☐

    e a company, to sell online courses to students ☐

    f a government department, to give guidelines for teaching ☐

1.2   **Which two urls are almost the same? How are they different?**

Task 2 Reading quickly for the main idea

Match each url from page 65 to one of the Internet pages below.

Source 1

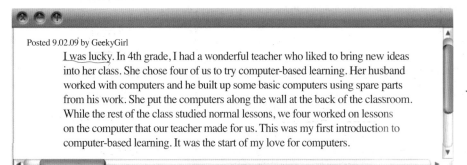

Posted 9.02.09 by GeekyGirl

I was lucky. In 4th grade, I had a wonderful teacher who liked to bring new ideas into her class. She chose four of us to try computer-based learning. Her husband worked with computers and he built up some basic computers using spare parts from his work. She put the computers along the wall at the back of the classroom. While the rest of the class studied normal lessons, we four worked on lessons on the computer that our teacher made for us. This was my first introduction to computer-based learning. It was the start of my love for computers.

Key words

spare parts

Source 2

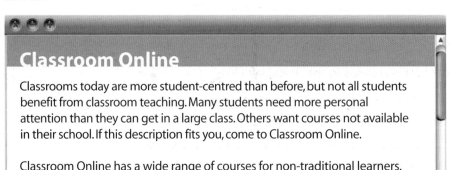

Classroom Online

Classrooms today are more student-centred than before, but not all students benefit from classroom teaching. Many students need more personal attention than they can get in a large class. Others want courses not available in their school. If this description fits you, come to Classroom Online.

Classroom Online has a wide range of courses for non-traditional learners. You can work independently or with an online tutor. You can choose different courses, including business and information technology (IT), or you can prepare for an English test online. You work at your own pace to complete each course.

Classroom Online does not provide high school credit, but our assessments are similar to standard exams and you get a certificate of completion with every course. We give you an official folder for your certificates so you can show them to potential employers.

Key words

student-centred
personal attention
description
non-traditional
independently
technology
your own pace
assessments
standard
a certificate
completion

Source 3

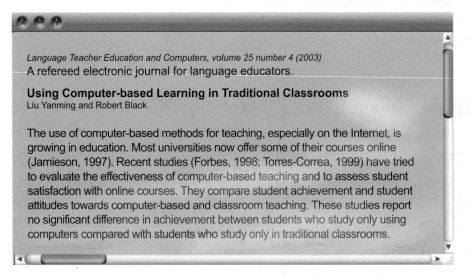

Language Teacher Education and Computers, volume 25 number 4 (2003)
A refereed electronic journal for language educators.

Using Computer-based Learning in Traditional Classrooms
Liu Yanming and Robert Black

The use of computer-based methods for teaching, especially on the Internet, is growing in education. Most universities now offer some of their courses online (Jamieson, 1997). Recent studies (Forbes, 1998; Torres-Correa, 1999) have tried to evaluate the effectiveness of computer-based teaching and to assess student satisfaction with online courses. They compare student achievement and student attitudes towards computer-based and classroom teaching. These studies report no significant difference in achievement between students who study only using computers compared with students who study only in traditional classrooms.

Key words

traditional
methods
especially
offer courses
recent studies
to assess
satisfaction
attitudes
significant
compared with

Source 4

Language Teacher Education and Computers, volume 30 number 2 (2008)
A refereed electronic journal for language educators.

Book review by Dr Lama Al-Khamees, Gateway University, Summerford
Computers in Language Classrooms
Pete Wu and Jing Wu
Roadhouse Publishers, London (2007)

Computers are important in our personal and professional lives. They now also play an important role in language classrooms. In recent years, publishers have provided new resources to use on computers, such as CDs and interactive software. Teachers have put materials on the Internet to supplement tasks and activities in language classrooms. In *Computers in Language Classrooms*, Pete Wu and Jing Wu have produced a guide that describes this new technology. The authors say that their purpose is to explain different kinds of computer-based learning to all language teachers who use computers. It is true that they provide a good introduction for new computer users, but the information may be too basic for more experienced users.

Key words

play a role

publishers

interactive software

materials

to supplement

activities

have produced a guide

too basic

Task 3 Reading carefully

For each source 1–4, try to answer the questions in the checklist below.

Purpose: Why has the information been published? Is it trying to sell ideas?

Viewpoint: Does it show many different views? Or does it show just one view?

Author: Is the author an expert in her/his subject? Has s/he published a lot of other books?

Quality: Has the information been checked by other experts?

Task 4 Thinking critically

How many questions from the checklist in Task 3 could you answer for each source? Which sources will be more reliable?

Task 5 Reading efficiently

5.1 **With other students, underline the main verbs in the sentences in Sources 1–4.**

5.2 **Find the noun phrase at the start of each sentence. What kind of noun does each one contain: *object noun, person noun, doing noun* or *idea noun*?**

Noticing grammar patterns

Noun phrases
In Units 2 and 3, you studied the following two noun phrase patterns:

noun phrase pattern	examples
noun + noun	*lecture theatre, computer laboratory*
doing noun + noun	*heating the mixture, washing the beans*

The academic texts in this lesson contain another kind of noun phrase:

noun phrase pattern	example
the + noun + *of* + noun + prepositional phrase	*the use of computer-based methods for teaching*

The third kind of noun phrase in the Noticing grammar patterns on page 67 is much longer than the other two. It has space for more ideas. It is often used when ideas are first introduced, to give more details.

The other noun phrases are shorter. They can be used to repeat ideas from the longer noun phrase later in the text. They give a summary of the ideas, so they do not need to contain all the information.

Example:

the use of computer-based methods for teaching → *computer-based teaching*

Task 6 Practising grammar patterns

Complete the related noun phrases below by writing suitable words in each gap.

The ideas in *italics* in the first column do not need to be repeated in columns 2 and 3.

introducing ideas *the* + noun + *of* + noun + prepositional phrase	summarizing ideas doing noun + noun	summarizing ideas noun + noun
a the use of computers *in classrooms*	_____ computers	computer _____
b _____ *computers* *for learning*	evaluating computers	_____ evaluation
c the _____ of teachers *by* *technology*	replacing _____	teacher replacement
d the introduction of technology *into* *classrooms*	_____ _____	technology introduction
e _____ *by a lecturer*	reviewing a book	a book review

Discussion

- Look again at Sources 1–4 on pages 66 and 67. Which sources have a formal style and which have an informal style? How do you know?

Task 7 Analyzing writing style

Look again at Sources 1–4. Use the information about noun phrases from Tasks 5 and 6 to help you think about the questions below.

a 1 Which sources mainly talk about ideas?
   2 Which ones mainly talk about people?

b 1 Which sources generally use long noun phrases as the starting point of sentences?
   2 Which ones use only short noun phrases?

Self study

Choose a text from the Internet or one that you have read in class. Analyze the style. Is it formal, informal, or a mixture of both? Find the noun phrases that are the subjects of the sentences. Decide if they name people, objects, activities/ processes or ideas. Which noun phrase pattern do they have? Compare the noun phrases in your text with the noun phrases in the table from Task 6.

Lesson 4

Choosing ideas from sources

Aims
- to recognize paraphrased ideas in original source texts
- to begin to understand conventions for referencing sources
- to understand the development of paragraphs from general to specific ideas

Chen has decided to use two sources that he found on the Internet for his assignment, because they are from an academic journal. He now needs to find ideas in the sources that he can use in his assignment. The question for his assignment is:
What are the advantages and disadvantages of computer-based learning compared with classroom learning?

Task 1 Reading quickly for the main idea

Look at the two sources from Lesson 3 on page 70. How many advantages and disadvantages of computer-based learning are mentioned in each source?

Task 2 Reading carefully to compare ideas

Look again at Sources 3 and 4. Look at the transcript from the conversation between Chen, Maysoun and Guy on page 206. Which advantages and disadvantages in the sources are similar to the ideas they discussed? Which ones are new?

Chen thinks he can use some ideas from the sources on page 70 in his assignment. He has to paraphrase the ideas, i.e., write them in different words from the original source, in order to fit his writing purpose. He also has to show very clearly in his assignment that the ideas are not his own, but are borrowed from sources. He does this by recording who published the ideas and when they were published.

Source 3

Language Teacher Education and Computers, volume 25 number 4 (2003)
A refereed electronic journal for language educators.

Using Computer-based Learning in Traditional Classrooms
Liu Yanming and Robert Black

The use of computer-based methods for teaching, especially on the Internet, is growing in education. Most universities now offer some of their courses online (Jamieson, 1997). Recent studies (Forbes, 1998; Torres-Correa, 1999) have tried to evaluate the effectiveness of computer-based teaching and to assess student satisfaction with online courses. They compare student achievement and student attitudes towards computer-based and classroom teaching. These studies report no significant difference in achievement between students who study only using computers compared with students who study only in traditional classrooms.

Several advantages of computer-based learning have been discussed. Jamieson (1997) found that online learning increased student numbers due to the convenience of studying at home. Torres-Correa (1999) reported that online learning was attractive for students with low incomes because it was less expensive. However, Jenkins (2000) carried out a survey of students who were studying and working at the same time. He found that some students had problems finding time to work and study. Others said that they missed the chance to work with other students or a tutor. Few studies have investigated the combination of computer-based and classroom learning. The purpose of this study is to assess the effectiveness of computer-based learning for improving independent learning in classrooms.

Key words

have been discussed

due to

attractive

low incomes

carried out

a survey

problems

missed

have investigated

the combination

independent

Source 4

Language Teacher Education and Computers, volume 30 number 2 (2008)
A refereed electronic journal for language educators.

Book review by Dr Lama Al-Khamees, Gateway University, Summerford
Computers in Language Classrooms
Pete Wu and Jing Wu, Roadhouse Publishers, London (2007)

Computers are important in our personal and professional lives. They now also play an important role in language classrooms. In recent years, publishers have provided new resources to use on computers, such as CDs and interactive software. Teachers have put materials on the Internet to supplement tasks and activities in language classrooms. In *Computers in Language Classrooms*, Pete Wu and Jing Wu have produced a guide that describes this new technology. The authors say that their purpose is to explain different kinds of computer-based learning to all language teachers who use computers. It is true that they provide a good introduction for new computer users, but the information may be too basic for more experienced users.

Computers in Language Classrooms consists of eight chapters that cover a wide range of topics – from using interactive software to making lessons on the Internet. The first chapter focuses on finding a balance between classroom teaching and computer-based teaching. Neither the computer nor the Internet will replace teachers, but technology can provide many benefits. These advantages include quick feedback for tasks, personal attention for learners and the development of independent learners. The authors also suggest that many language learners expect computers in the classroom because they have grown up with technology and understand how to use it.

Key words

consists of

a balance

neither ... nor

will replace

the development

Task 3 Reading carefully to identify ideas

Match the paraphrased ideas, a–j, to the person or people who published these ideas, 1–6. Write the correct number in each box. Then add the date that the ideas were published. The first one has been done for you.

Paraphrased ideas	Source	Date
a Computers can provide benefits such as giving answers to tasks quickly.	6	2007
b Students who do not have much money prefer computer-based learning.		_____
c There are few studies that evaluate computer-based learning in classrooms.		_____
d Many students now know how to use computers, so they expect to see them in classrooms.		_____
e Students who learn on computers achieve similar grades to students who learn in classrooms.		_____
f Computers will not replace teachers, but they can help students to become more independent learners.		_____
g Online learning is more convenient because students can study at home.		_____
h Many universities offer online courses.		_____
i Some students have difficulty working and studying at the same time.		_____
j Some students prefer to work with a tutor or other students.		_____

1 Forbes; Torres-Correa

2 Jamieson

3 Jenkins

4 Torres-Correa

5 Liu Yanming and Robert Black

6 Pete Wu and Jing Wu

Noticing language

General and specific ideas

General ideas apply to a wide range of situations or people, whereas specific ideas apply to only one or a small number of situations or people.

General

Classrooms today are more student-centred than before. (Applies to all classrooms)

Many students need more personal attention. (Applies to many students)

Specific

I was lucky. I had a wonderful teacher. (Applies to one person: GeekyGirl)

This was my first introduction to computer-based learning. (Applies to one person: GeekyGirl)

Task 4 Reading efficiently

Look at the introductions (i.e., the first paragraph) to the two sources on page 70, and answer the questions below.

a Which sentence in each introduction contains the most general idea?

b Which sentence in each introduction contains the most specific idea?

c Complete the statements below.

1 The sentences in the middle of these paragraphs are more specific than

_____ .

2 The sentences in the middle of these paragraphs are less specific than

_____ .

d How does this organization help a reader?

Task 5 Thinking critically

Think about your answers from Task 4. Are introductions to academic texts organized like this in your language?

Task 6 Organizing a text

Below are some sentences which summarize the ideas from the two texts on page 70. Work with other students to put the ideas in order, from general to specific. Write a number from 1 (most general) to 7 (most specific) in each box.

a Many language classrooms have computers with access to the Internet.

b A new study has investigated the effectiveness of using computers in classrooms.

c It is true that some students prefer to study online because it is cheaper and more convenient.

d Computers and the Internet are important tools for studying language.

e However, others like the social aspect of studying in classrooms.

f Some teachers worry that their jobs will disappear because computers will replace them.

g Many language courses are now available online.

> **Self study**
>
> Search on the Internet to find an academic text in your language. Look at the introduction. Does it have the same kind of organization as an introduction in English?

Lesson 5
Using the information you find

Aims
- to show a viewpoint clearly in writing
- to organize ideas so a reader can understand them
- to use and acknowledge sources of information correctly

Chen is ready to write his assignment. He needs to choose a viewpoint to help him organize his ideas. The question for Chen's assignment is: *What are the advantages and disadvantages of computer-based learning compared with classroom learning?*

Discussion
- Look at the conversation transcript on page 206. Does Chen prefer learning in classrooms or computer-based learning?

feature	computer-based learning	classroom learning
convenience	You can study any time.	You have to study at specific times.
time	You have to set your own deadlines.	The teacher sets deadlines.
cost	You can study at home.	You may have to travel.
flexibility	You can keep your job.	You may have to give up your job.
social group	You cannot see people.	You can see people to discuss ideas.
fluency	You can take time to think what to say.	You have to speak quickly.

In Lesson 1, Chen created the table of ideas above for his assignment. He has now reorganized the table and redrafted some reasons to show his preference clearly. Chen's new table is below.

feature	computer-based learning	classroom learning
cost	you can study at home	you may have to travel
convenience	you can study any time	you have to study at specific times
	you can set your own deadlines	you have to meet deadlines
flexibility	you can keep your job	you may have to give up your job
social group	you cannot see people	you can see people to discuss ideas
	you can take time to think what to say	you have to speak quickly

Task 1 Organizing ideas

1.1 Look at Chen's *new* table of ideas on page 73. What changes has he made?

1.2 Look at the subject noun and verb at the starting point of each sentence in columns 2 and 3 of the table. Answer the questions below.

   a Which column mainly shows the type of learning as an advantage, i.e., a positive viewpoint?

   b Which column mainly shows the type of learning as a disadvantage, i.e., a negative viewpoint?

Task 2 Thinking critically

Which comparison in Chen's new table does not support his viewpoint? Should Chen include this comparison in his assignment? How can he deal with it?

Comparing and contrasting ideas

Look back to Lesson 1, Task 9, where you wrote some claims and supported them with reasons.

Example:

Computer-based learning is more convenient than classroom learning, because you can study any time and you can take more time if you need to.

Look back to Lesson 2, Task 6, where you joined sentences to show contrasts. You can do the same for the sentences in the table on page 73.

Example:

Computer-based learning is cheap, whereas classroom learning can be expensive because you may have to travel in order to study.

Task 3 Reviewing grammar patterns

3.1 Use the two grammar patterns above to write some more comparisons and contrasts for Chen's assignment. Look at the table on page 73 for ideas.

3.2 Work in pairs. Use the checklist below to evaluate your claims.
   - Do your sentences clearly show Chen's viewpoint?
   - Do your sentences include the basis for the comparison or contrast?
   - Do you give reasons for your claims?
   - Do your sentences use the language patterns correctly?

Task 4 Organizing a text

Chen has to decide how to organize his assignment in order to show his viewpoint clearly.

Look back to Lesson 2, Task 4 to remember how the librarian organized her ideas to contrast libraries and the Internet. Which of the patterns listed below should Chen choose?

a Describe computer-based learning and classroom learning separately and list all their features.

b Take each feature in turn and compare computer-based learning and classroom learning on the basis of just that feature.

c Describe the advantages of computer-based learning and then the disadvantages.

Chen needs an introduction for his assignment. In Lesson 4, Task 4, you studied the general to specific development of introductions. This helps readers to build a picture of the ideas in their minds.

Task 5 Thinking critically

Below are the first sentences from the introductions to Sources 2, 3 and 4 in Lesson 3.

Could Chen use one of the sentences below for the introduction to his assignment? Give reasons for your answer.

a *Classrooms today are more student-centred than before, but not all students benefit from classroom teaching.*

b *The use of computer-based methods for teaching, especially on the Internet, is growing in education.*

c *Computers are important in our personal and professional lives.*

Task 6 Writing an introduction

Chen's introduction develops from general to specific ideas. It has to prepare readers for the ideas in his second paragraph. The final sentence tells readers which features Chen will use in his comparison.

Read Chen's second paragraph, below, and complete the introduction.

Nowadays, students can choose **(a)** _____. Sometimes, these two kinds of learning **(b)** _____. There are advantages and disadvantages **(c)** _____. I will compare **(d)** _____ in terms of **(e)** _____.

Below is the second paragraph of Chen's assignment. In this paragraph, he compares computer-based learning and classroom learning. He has put in some numbers to show where he wants to use information from his sources. He will include this information later, once he has written his own ideas.

Many students prefer online courses because they are cheaper. Students can study at home and they do not have to travel. (2) Learning online is more convenient. than learning in a traditional classroom because it is more flexible. Students can study and work at the same time. (3) They can set their own deadlines and take more time if they need to. Students with an advanced level usually prefer classrooms because they like to discuss their work with other students and the tutor. However, students with a low level cannot speak quickly. They usually prefer online discussions because they can take time to think what to say. (4)

Task 7 Thinking critically

Work in pairs to compare your introductions from Task 6. Are they helpful for a reader? Tell your partner something you like about her/his paragraph and something you think s/he could improve.

Chen wants to include some information from his sources to show that he has read and understood their ideas. In order to do that, he has to summarize the ideas to fit into his assignment.

Task 8 Using the ideas of other writers

Chen has borrowed the ideas below from academic sources to support his ideas.

a Studies show 'no significant difference in achievement' for students in both kinds of learning (Liu and Black, 2003).

b Putting courses on the Internet means more students with low incomes can afford them (Torres–Correa, 1999, cited in Liu and Black, 2003).

c It is true that some students have problems studying and working (Jenkins, 2000, cited in Liu and Black, 2003).

d Wu and Wu (2007, cited in Al–Khamees, 2008) suggest that computers will not replace teachers but they can help students to become more independent learners.

8.1 Find the information in the texts on page 70 that Chen decided to use, and match it to his summaries above. How did Chen change the information from the sources in order to write in his own words?

8.2 Look back at the paragraph on page 75. Chen wrote numbers in his assignment to show where he wanted to use source information from. Where possible, write a number, 2–4, from the paragraph next to the correct summary, a–d, above.

8.3 Which one of the summaries a–d could fit into your introduction from Task 6? Where would you put it?

8.4 Look again at the paragraph on page 75. Now that it contains information from the sources, it could be divided to make more paragraphs. Where would you divide it? How many paragraphs would you make?

Task 9 Thinking critically

9.1 Why does sentence a in Task 8 have inverted commas around 'no significant difference in achievement'?

9.2 Why do references b, c and d include cited in Liu and Black or cited in Al-Khamees?

Self study

Choose another question for an assignment.

Example: What are the advantages and disadvantages of working in groups compared with working on your own?

Brainstorm ideas and organize them into a table to show the features that your comparisons are based on. Decide on your viewpoint and write sentences to show it. Use the features to organize your paragraphs. Find some sources with more ideas that you could include in your assignment.

Unit 5

New ideas and new concepts

Lesson 1

Quick explanations

Aims
- to think about the pressure of studying new topics at university
- to understand how lecturers and writers explain new technical terms quickly and simply
- to write simple explanations of technical terms

The start of a new course is a time for understanding new ways of doing things and for understanding new concepts. Maysoun has been thinking about this aspect of university study. She writes about it in her English diary, where she writes two or three times each week to try to improve her English.

Key words

concepts
aspect
diary
to improve

Task 1 Reading quickly for the main idea

Read the first paragraph of Maysoun's thoughts and feelings about starting a new course, below. Tick ✓ the two best adjectives to describe what she thinks.

a important

b practical

c exciting

d worrying

e international

f interesting

<u>Semester 1, week 4, Tuesday</u>

It is very exciting to learn about new topics at university. Guy, for example, is excited about his marketing module because he would like to work in international marketing when he graduates. Chen's software development practical classes are exciting for him because the tutors have so many new ideas to help him to write better programs. I am very excited that I am doing Dr Charles' module called 'Water in the environment' because she is an important international specialist in the field. But we are all feeling some pressure at the moment. There are some things about learning the new modules that make us feel worried.

Key words

topics
exciting
feeling pressure
worried

Task 2 Reading carefully for specific information

Look again at the diary extract above. Find reasons why the students are excited about their courses. Write the correct student's name next to each reason below.

a because this module is highly relevant to this student's personal plans for the future _____

b because this module is delivered by a world expert _____

c because this module is providing new ways to improve essential skills _____

Discussion

- Maysoun writes about pressure in her diary. What do you think are her main worries about learning new topics at university?

Task 3 Reading carefully to understand

After your discussion, read the next paragraph of Maysoun's diary, below, to see if you are correct.

There are so many unfamiliar technical terms to learn. Guy says this is true even for students who have English as their first language. This new technical vocabulary is a heavy workload and it comes very quickly in the first few days. At the same time, we get details of all the assignments for the module topic, and this is another heavy load of things to read and things to write. I feel less confident now than in week one!

I can remember having this bad feeling in my first year of Geography BSc. But I learnt to manage the vocabulary workload by reviewing my notes from lectures and books so that I could add the new words to my vocabulary notebooks and check their meanings carefully. I also learnt to listen and read carefully to catch meanings, because lecturers often put them right next to the technical terms, and you can miss them.

Key words

technical terms
a heavy workload
confident
to manage
reviewing
catch meanings

Task 4 Studying smart

Look again at the extract from Maysoun's diary above. Notice how she managed the large number of new words that she needed when she was an undergraduate. Use her ideas to make a checklist for yourself, or complete the list below.

Personal checklist for managing new vocabulary

1 _____ carefully in lectures to notice when a lecturer gives _____ of words.

2 _____ my lecture notes.

3 _____ carefully to notice when a writer gives _____ of words.

4 Find exact _____ of new technical terms.

5 Record them in my _____ _____ .

Task 5 Listening

⊙CD1-16 Listen again to the extract from Dr Charles' lecture about the water cycle, and complete the exercises below.

a Write down three technical terms that Dr Charles explains, together with their explanations.

b Write down two technical terms that Dr Charles does not explain.

c Read the transcript on page 208 to check your answers. Are there any more technical terms that you do not understand? Are they explained or not?

Task 6 Listening for explanations

◉CD1-17 Listen to the extract from Chen's lecture about software development, and complete the exercises below.

a Write down two technical terms that are explained, together with their explanations.

b Write down one technical term that is not explained. Can you guess what it means?

c Read the transcript on page 208 to check your answers.

Noticing language patterns

Using synonyms to explain meaning

Lecturers and writers often explain technical terms quickly using another word or phrase that means the same. These are called *synonyms*.

The table below shows language patterns for using synonyms to explain the meaning of a term.

pattern	example
commas	*Next, the code, the computer program, is written.*
brackets	*Next, the code (the computer program) is written.*
, or ...,	*Next, the code, or the computer program, is written.*
, i.e., ...,	*Next, the code, i.e., the computer program, is written.*

Task 7 Practising language patterns

Write synonyms to explain the underlined terms in the extracts below. Use any of the patterns from the box above.

a Then we'll start looking at the different stages in the cycle in much more detail, in particular at the roles played by <u>geology</u> and <u>vegetation</u> in the process.

_____

_____

b At this stage, each programmer's purpose is to make the program efficient, adaptable and <u>bug-free</u>.

_____

_____

Synonyms

You can find synonyms to explain word meanings in dictionaries and in word-processing software. Synonyms are a quick and useful way to explain the meanings of words, but they are not always precise, i.e., exact, meanings. In addition, a word can have more than one meaning and therefore more than one synonym. You need to check how the word is being used in order to find the synonym with the closest meaning.

Task 8 Noticing meaning

The word *gather* has several synonyms, including *meet*, *get together* and *collect*.

8.1 **Which synonym is correct for the sentence below, taken from the Unit 3 transcript on page 205?**

In the first stage, the requirements for the system are <u>gathered</u> by talking to the customer and other people who will use it.

8.2 **Tick ☑ the correct synonym for the underlined word in each sentence below.**

a <u>Key</u> words are words that students will need to know for their academic studies.

☐ answer ☐ important ☐ enter

b Universities have to provide academic courses that are up to date, challenging and prepare you to be a professional in your <u>field</u>.

☐ sports ground ☐ specialist area ☐ grassland

c When I started to <u>struggle</u> with the work, I didn't want to tell anyone.

☐ resist ☐ fight ☐ have problems

d <u>Secure</u> the cylinder with the elastic band.

☐ fix ☐ safe ☐ protect

e I hope I've <u>convinced</u> you that the library is a good place to find information.

☐ sure ☐ certain ☐ persuaded

8.3 **Where possible, explain why the synonyms you have not chosen would be incorrect in the sentence.**

Task 9 Finding synonyms

As quickly as you can, find a synonym for each of the key words below, taken from previous units. Say it aloud and write it down.

Unit 1		Unit 3	
vacation	_____	stages	_____
sufficient	_____	hazards	_____
global	_____	essential	_____
completed	_____	data	_____

Unit 2		Unit 4	
location	_____	locate	_____
participate	_____	evaluate	_____
familiar	_____	benefits (n)	_____
improve	_____	significant	_____

Self study

Where can you find the precise (exact) meanings of new technical terms? Find synonyms to explain three technical terms in your subject area, and share them with another student. Make sure you know how to find synonyms of non-technical words using the word-processing software on the computers you use.

Lesson 2
Shared concepts

Aims
- to understand the purpose of definitions
- to understand the general to specific structure of definitions
- to understand and use language patterns for functional definitions

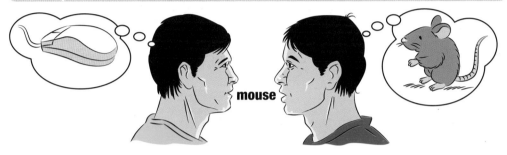

mouse

At university, students have to learn many new academic concepts with their technical terms (their names). Each concept has to be carefully explained and linked to its term using a definition. Definitions are longer, more detailed explanations than synonyms. They explain clearly and precisely what a term means. As well as understanding these new terms, students have to write clear, precise definitions in their assignments and examinations to show that they understand the important concepts in their subjects.

Task 1 Understanding definitions

Match each term a–h with its definition 1–8. Write the correct number in each box. The first one has been done for you.

a An expert   3

b Machine code

c A bug

d Constructive feedback

e A pathogen

f A computer mouse

g A market survey

h A subject-specific term

1 is comments about what is good and what can be improved.

2 is an organism that can cause disease in another organism.

3 is a person who has studied a subject deeply for a long time.

4 is a mistake in a computer program that stops the program doing what it should do.

5 is a word or phrase that is used in one subject area but not in others, or that has a different meaning in different subject areas.

6 is a system of instructions that computers can follow.

7 is a device for converting hand movements into digital signals.

8 is research to gather information about consumers, products and services.

Key words
an organism
a device
converting
digital signals
a market survey
consumers
products
services

Noticing language patterns

The structure of definitions

A definition usually has the following pattern:

term + *is* + general noun + specific feature

term	*is*	general noun	specific feature
a computer mouse	is	a device	for converting hand movements into digital signals.
an expert	is	a person	who has studied a subject deeply for a long time.

In a definition, the general noun tells you the class (group) that the term belongs to, e.g., a person or a device. However, there are many different kinds of people and devices. You need a specific feature to give a more precise meaning.

Task 2 Practising language patterns

Without referring back to Task 1, complete the table below with a suitable general noun and specific feature for each term.

term	*is*	general (class) noun	specific feature
a An expert	is	a _____	who has _____ a subject deeply for a long time.
b A computer mouse		a _____	for _____ hand movements into digital signals.
c A bug	is	a _____	in a computer program that _____ the program doing what it should do.
d A subject-specific term	is	a _____ or _____	that is used in one subject area _____, or that has a different _____ in different subject areas.
e A market survey	is	_____	to _____ about consumers, products and services.
f A pathogen	is	an _____	that can cause _____ in another organism.

Task 3 Thinking critically

Which two of the definitions above tell you the intended purpose or function of the term (what it is supposed to do)?

Noticing grammar patterns

Language for functional definitions

In functional definitions, the specific feature is the purpose of something or its function (what it does): *A market survey is research to gather information about consumers, products and services.*

Notice that purpose is given by the pattern for a purpose statement: `to + verb`

In the next example, a computer mouse is defined by its function, i.e., what it does: *A computer mouse is a device for converting hand movements into digital signals.*

Notice that function is given by the pattern for a function statement: `for + doing noun`

Sometimes, the general noun is already in the term being defined, so it has to be repeated. The word *machine* has to be used twice in this definition:

A washing machine is a machine for washing clothes.

Task 4 Writing definitions

4.1 Write functional definitions for the terms below, which were used in earlier units.

> a lab coat   a fire alarm   a personal statement
> a vocabulary notebook   Freshers' Week

4.2 From your general knowledge, write functional definitions for the terms below.

> an umbrella   a scanner   an ATM   debugging   a web browser

4.3 Compare your definitions with other students and try to improve them.

Task 5 Noticing language and thinking critically

Look at the academic definitions 1–8, and answer the questions below.

The definitions are from courses studied by Guy (International Business), Chen (Computer Science) and Maysoun (Environmental Studies).

a Identify the academic subject for each definition and give your reasons.

b Look at the general nouns in the definitions. Which of them are used in more than one academic subject?

1 The World Wide Web is a system of interlinked documents which can be accessed via the Internet using a web browser.

2 Privatization is the process through which an organization goes if it passes from public (state) ownership to private ownership.

3 Titration is the process in a laboratory for finding the concentration of solutions.

4 The Retail Prices Index is a measure of the rate of inflation.

5 A USB is a device to connect peripherals to a computer using wires.

6 Encryption is a process for converting plaintext, or normal text, into ciphertext.

7 pH is a measure of the concentration of H+ ions in solution.

8 BOD (biochemical oxygen demand) is a measure of the polluting capacity of an effluent due to the dissolved oxygen taken up by microorganisms as they decompose the organic matter in the effluent.

Noticing language patterns

General to specific

The definition of a term moves from the general noun to increasingly specific information, often in prepositional phrases.

term	is/are	general noun	specific information	more specific information	even more specific information
The World Wide Web	is	a system	of interlinked documents	which can be accessed using a web browser	via the Internet.

Task 6 Practising language patterns: general to specific

Cover the language pattern example above. Without referring to the definitions from Task 5, put the phrases below into the correct order to reconstruct them.

a The World Wide Web is   via the Internet   a system   which can be accessed of interlinked documents   using a web browser

_____

_____

b Privatization is   from public (state) ownership to private ownership the process   if it passes   through which an organization goes

_____

_____

c Titration is   for finding the concentration   a process   of solutions in a laboratory

_____

_____

d The Retail Prices Index is   of inflation   of the rate   a measure

_____

e A USB is   to connect peripherals to a computer   a device   using wires

_____

f Encryption is   into ciphertext   for converting plaintext or normal text   a process

_____

g pH is   in solution   of the concentration of H+ ions   a measure

_____

h BOD (biochemical oxygen demand) is   due to the dissolved oxygen   of the polluting capacity   taken up by microorganisms   a measure   as they decompose the organic matter in the effluent   of an effluent

_____

_____

Self study

Find useful functional definitions in a specialist dictionary for your subject and add them to your vocabulary notebook. Underline the purpose statements and the function statements. Notice how they are organized from general to specific information.

Lesson 3
Working with formal definitions

Aims
- to understand and use language patterns for formal definitions
- to critically evaluate definitions

Maysoun has to write about pollution for one of her assignments, *Compare and contrast pollution in an urban and a rural community*. She decides that she needs to start with a clear definition of the term *pollution*.

Discussion
- Brainstorm the meaning of *pollution*. For each of your ideas, write down a general noun and a specific feature.

Because pollution doesn't have a purpose or a function, Maysoun can't use the pattern for a functional definition. Instead, she decides to use a formal definition.

Noticing grammar patterns

Definitions using relative pronouns
In formal definitions, the specific feature starts with a relative pronoun, i.e., *that, which[1], where, who* or *when*.

Task 1 Noticing grammar patterns: formal definitions

1.1 **Underline the relative pronoun in each definition below.**

a Machine code is a system of instructions that computers can follow.

b A pathogen is an organism which can cause disease in another organism.

c An expert is a person who has studied the subject deeply for a long time.

d A noticeboard is a place where people can leave messages.

e A deadline is a date when an assignment must be handed in.

1.2 **Complete the language pattern table below.**

noun	relative pronoun
person	*that or* _____
place	*that or* _____
time	*that or* _____
thing	*that or* _____
concept	*that or* _____

Task 2 Thinking critically: definitions

Maysoun's first draft is: *Pollution is chemicals that pollute the environment.*

What do you think is wrong with Maysoun's definition? How can you improve it?

[1] In American English, *that* is used as the relative pronoun in definitions of thing nouns, not *which*. In British English, *that* is usually used in speaking.

On page 85, Maysoun tried to explain the term *pollution* using the verb *pollutes*, which is from the same word family. This is not useful. It is called a *circular definition*, because it makes the reader go round the word family in a circle, getting nowhere.

In general English, *pollution* can refer to *chemicals*, but this is too specific for Maysoun's assignment. She needs a more accurate, scientific definition with a better general noun that can include all the ideas she wants to develop for the assignment, such as different kinds of pollution, what causes pollution and what the effects are.

Study smart

Study the definitions checklist below.

- Don't write a circular definition.
- Don't forget to use a suitable general noun.
- Don't forget to explain the specific feature.

Task 3 Thinking critically: improving definitions

3.1 Check your definition from Task 2 with another student. Is it circular? Is your general noun more suitable for Maysoun's assignment than *chemicals*?

3.2 The statements below are all true, but which one is a successful definition?

a Pathogens can kill living things.

b A web browser is a computer program.

c Effluent results from human activities and pollutes rivers.

d Open-access computer labs are places where students from any department within the university can use computers.

e Verification is a stage in the software development process.

f In the software development process, verification is the stage for verifying the software.

3.3 Say what is wrong with the other definitions above. Choose from the following:

no general noun   no specific feature   circular

3.4 Rewrite the unsuccessful definitions to improve them.

Task 4 Writing definitions

4.1 Write definitions using relative pronouns for the terms below, from earlier units.

a computer programmer   collocations   a draft   a health centre
a supervisor   a library   office hours

4.2 Check your definitions with another student and give feedback.

Task 5 Thinking critically

Sometimes, the specific feature in a definition of a term is not specific enough. It does not make the term clearly different from other, similar terms.

In what ways are the definitions below not specific enough?

a A computer mouse is a device for converting hand movements into digital signals.

b Experts are people who have studied a subject deeply for a long time.

Self study

Find definitions in your subject area and list the general nouns used. Decide with other students which general nouns are transferable to other subjects and which are subject–specific.

Lesson 4
Analyzing concepts

Aims
- to understand how new concepts are explained by definition and analysis
- to learn language for analyzing concepts
- to explain concepts by defining and analyzing them using tree diagrams

Pollution is a very familiar concept. However, in an academic course such as Environmental Studies, a concept has to be carefully defined and analyzed. Maysoun is trying to do this in a draft introductory section for an assignment, *Compare and contrast the effects of pollution in an urban and a rural community.*

Task 1 Thinking critically

Maysoun's final draft of the definition of pollution is: *Pollution is a process which puts unwanted materials or energy into an environment.*

1.1 In what ways is it better than her first draft, *Pollution is chemicals that pollute the environment*?

1.2 Is Maysoun's definition of pollution different from the one you wrote in Lesson 3? Which is better, yours or hers? Why?

Task 2 Reading quickly for text organization

Read Maysoun's introduction on page 88 quickly. Answer the questions below.

a How many different types of analysis will she describe in her assignment?

b What is the purpose of the first paragraph?

Task 3 Reading carefully for details

Read Maysoun's introduction carefully and answer the questions below.

a What are the two related concepts that are defined in paragraph 1?

b What are the purposes of paragraphs 2 and 3?

c What will be the purposes of the next two paragraphs?

Compare and contrast the effects of pollution in an urban and a rural community

Introduction

Pollution is a process which puts unwanted materials or energy into an environment. These unwanted items are called 'pollutants' or 'contaminants'. They are unwanted for the reason that they make ecological systems in the environment unstable and may damage the environment and its organisms.

The concept of pollution can be analyzed in different ways. First, pollution can be described in terms of the pollutants. It can also be classified according to the type of environment that is polluted. Sometimes, pollution is classified by the sources of the pollutants. These three approaches will be described.

Pollution can be described in terms of three general categories of pollutants: pathogens, non-biological materials and energy. Pathogens are any organisms that cause disease to other organisms. Many diseases, such as cholera, are caused by pathogen pollution of water. The non-biological materials can be further subdivided into two categories: particulates and chemicals. Particulates are very small pieces of material, including dust and fibres. Chemicals can pollute as gases, e.g., CO_2 (carbon dioxide), liquids, e.g., detergents, and solids, e.g., metals such as iron. Energy is a pollutant when excess heat, light or noise enters the environment.

Key words

an urban
community

a rural community

unwanted

energy

are called

the pollutants

contaminants

ecological

unstable

may damage

can be analyzed

can be classified

approaches

cholera

non-biological

can be further
subdivided

particulates

dust

fibres

gases

carbon dioxide

detergents

solids

metals

iron

excess

Task 4 Reading and note taking

You are going to make notes on the concept of pollutants, using the information from the introduction above.

4.1   Which paragraphs of the introduction will be relevant?

4.2   Complete the definition and the notes in the tree diagram below.

Definition: Pollutants are unwanted _____ and _____ in an environment.

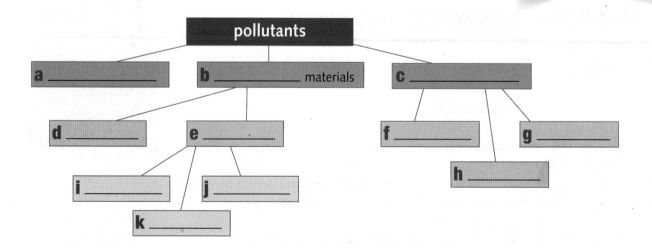

Discussion

- Do you agree with Maysoun's analysis of the concept of pollution so far? Is it clear and logical? Can you think of more examples of pollutants, from your own experience?

Task 5 Noticing key language

Look again at the introduction on page 88. Find and list key words for defining and analyzing a concept and for giving examples. Compare your list with another student.

Noticing grammar patterns

Maysoun's analysis explains three systems for classifying pollution. Paragraph 2 gives the basis of each different classification system.

pattern	example
preposition + noun phrase	*in terms of the pollutants*

Task 6 Noticing grammar patterns

Complete a–c, below, showing language for the basis of analysis or classification. The information is taken from paragraph 2 of the introduction on page 88.

	preposition	noun phrase
a	in _____ of	the pollutants
b	_____ to	the type of environment that is polluted
c	_____	the sources of the pollutants

Task 7 Writing practice

Look at Maysoun's notes for paragraph 4, below. They are in the form of a tree diagram. Use them to complete the draft paragraph below.

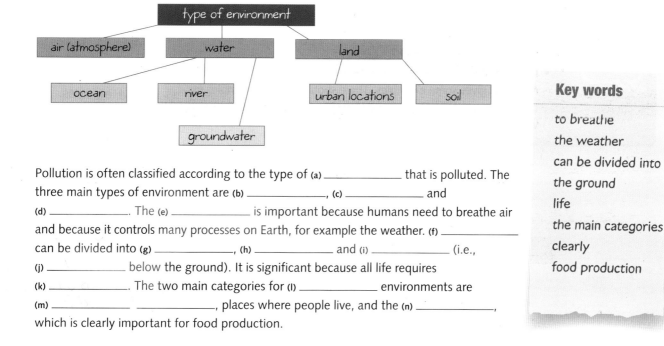

Pollution is often classified according to the type of (a) _____ that is polluted. The three main types of environment are (b) _____, (c) _____ and (d) _____. The (e) _____ is important because humans need to breathe air and because it controls many processes on Earth, for example the weather. (f) _____ can be divided into (g) _____, (h) _____ and (i) _____ (i.e., (j) _____ below the ground). It is significant because all life requires (k) _____. The two main categories for (l) _____ environments are (m) _____ _____, places where people live, and the (n) _____, which is clearly important for food production.

Key words

to breathe

the weather

can be divided into

the ground

life

the main categories

clearly

food production

Task 9 Understanding the writer's purpose

Because Chen couldn't go to the lecture, Guy has summarized the information for him.

Look at Guy's summary of the lecture, below, and answer the questions.

a Where is the definition given?

b Where is the classification system explained?

The Dewey Decimal system is a system for classifying information sources such as books and journals. The information is classified on the basis of topics and uses a base 10 numbering system to label general categories and subcategories. At the lowest and most specific level of the system, books are arranged alphabetically according to authors' family names.

Task 10 Noticing language

Find key words for classification in Guy's summary, above. Add them to the right-hand column of the table in Task 8.

Task 11 Practising language

11.1 Complete the description of a supermarket and its organization below. Write suitable words and phrases in the gaps.

A supermarket is a store (a) _____ the goods, usually food and other household Items, are collected by customers before they are purchased. To help the customers to find the goods, they are (b) _____ in general (c) _____, such as vegetables, freezer goods and canned goods, and then (d) _____ subcategories, (e) _____ canned vegetables and canned fruit. At the lowest and most (f) _____ level of the system, some goods are grouped by the brand and some are arranged (g) _____ price.

11.2 Find another key phrase and key word from the text above and add them to the table in Task 8. One has been done for you.

> **Key words**
>
> a store
> household items
> customers
> are purchased
> freezer goods
> are grouped
> the brand

> ### Self study
>
> Write a short text to explain how the students, courses or books in your school, college or university are organized, or about how music and films (DVDs) are arranged in a store near you. Use the language in the table from Task 8.

Mid-course review

Look back through the work you have done in Units 1–5. Tick ✓ or cross ✗ each *I can* ... statement below. Add a comment if you wish. Go back and review the topics you have put a cross by.

Unit 1 I can ...	writing	speaking	comment
name my academic subject(s)			
make purpose statements			
complete a form			
use examples to support purpose statements			

Unit 2 I can ...	writing	speaking	comment
describe position (where something is)			
describe a school or university campus			
ask about someone's name			
make a study plan			
give constructive feedback to another student			

Unit 3 I can ...	writing	speaking	comment
ask questions in a lecture			
describe purpose (why?) and method (how?)			
describe a process from instructions			
describe a process from a flow diagram			
make notes in a flow diagram			

Unit 4 I can ...	writing	speaking	comment
brainstorm ideas with other students			
evaluate sources using a checklist			
organize my ideas in a table based on features			
write sentences to compare and contrast			
organize a text from general to specific ideas			
recognize noun phrases in a text			

Unit 5 I can ...	writing	speaking	comment
say numbers			
use synonyms to explain a word			
give a definition			
explain a classification system from a tree diagram			
make notes in a tree diagram			

Lesson 1

Exploring change and development

Aims

- to experiment with strategies for listening for key information
- to take notes about change over time using a timeline
- to understand and use language patterns for situations, trends and events

Chen, Maysoun and Guy have been busy on their courses and they have not seen each other for a while. Guy suggests they go together to a talk about the history of Gateway University. Guy has a special interest in the history of the university, because some of his family members also studied there.

Task 1 Listening

Guy shows Maysoun and Chen some photos of his family members and talks about their connection with Gateway University.

1.1 **Decide whether you want to read and listen, or just listen, to what Guy says. See page 210 for the transcript.**

1.2 **⊙ CD1-20 Listen to what Guy says. Write two key events in his family history on the timeline below.**

College founded   _____ _____

| | | | |
| 1860 | | 1960 | 1980 | Now |

Discussion

- Guy talked about his family and the times they were at the university. The lecturer will give more general information about the history of the university. What other topics do you think the lecturer will talk about?

Task 2 Listening and making notes

Guy wants to remember the key dates and events from the talk, because he thinks his parents will be interested in the history of Gateway University. He asks Chen and Maysoun to help him take notes.

⊚CD1-21 **Listen to the talk, working with a partner to take notes. One of you should listen for the key dates or times mentioned. The other should listen for the key events. Record your notes on the timeline below.**

Timeline

12th century	Oxford and Cambridge Universities founded
_____	_____
_____	_____
_____	_____
20th century	_____
_____	university status
_____	

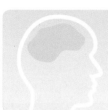

Study smart

Discuss your notes with your partner to complete the timeline from Task 2. Did you find it useful to focus on just one type of information? Is this strategy helpful for listening?

Task 3 Thinking critically

3.1 In Task 2, did you note the dates and personal information about the speaker? Is this information relevant to the general history of the university? Why did the speaker include this information?

3.2 Compare the two timelines on this page and page 97. Which of Guy's facts, below, were incorrect? Put a cross ☒ beside the incorrect facts.

a Gateway University started as a working-class college.

b It was intended for people to learn to read and write properly.

c It started in the 1860s.

Task 4 Reviewing and extending language patterns

George Blackstone and Guy both talk about periods of time, specific points in time and sequences in time.

Look at the transcripts on pages 210 and 211. Find phrases to add to the table below.

period of time (duration)	point in time	sequence in time
in the 80s	in 1967	after it was set up

Task 5 Thinking critically

Which phrases in the table above give a specific time, and which phrases give an approximate time? Why do the speakers choose to give specific or approximate times?

Task 6 Noticing grammar patterns

Both Guy and George Blackstone talk about general situations, or trends, and specific events in the history of the university. Examples from Guy's conversation are shown in the table below.

6.1 Look at the transcript of the talk by George Blackstone on pages 210 and 211 and try to find more examples of these patterns. Write them in the table.

6.2 Underline the verb and say what form it has, e.g., *present simple*.

purpose	example	verb form
General situation: to describe unchanging situations in the present or in the past	This is my mum and dad at their graduation. His family <u>were</u> working class.	present simple past simple
General trend: to look back over the past from the present	My family <u>has been involved</u> with Gateway for quite a long time.	present perfect
Specific event: to describe events or actions	Some members of my family <u>studied</u> here. It <u>started</u> as a college for working-class people.	past simple

Task 7 Practising grammar patterns

Guy writes an e-mail to his parents about the history of the university.

Write the correct form of the verb in brackets in each gap.

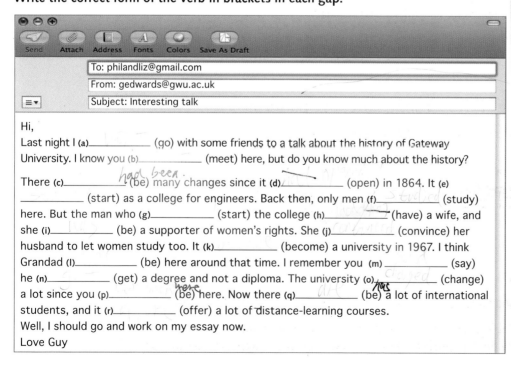

To: philandliz@gmail.com
From: gedwards@gwu.ac.uk
Subject: Interesting talk

Hi,
Last night I (a)_____ (go) with some friends to a talk about the history of Gateway University. I know you (b)_____ (meet) here, but do you know much about the history?
There (c)___had been___ (be) many changes since it (d)_____ (open) in 1864. It (e) _____ (start) as a college for engineers. Back then, only men (f)___studied___ (study) here. But the man who (g)_____ (start) the college (h)_____ (have) a wife, and she (i)_____ (be) a supporter of women's rights. She (j)_____ (convince) her husband to let women study too. It (k)_____ (become) a university in 1967. I think Grandad (l)_____ (be) here around that time. I remember you (m)_____ (say) he (n)_____ (get) a degree and not a diploma. The university (o)___has___ (change) a lot since you (p)___here___ (be) here. Now there (q)___are___ (be) a lot of international students, and it (r)_____ (offer) a lot of distance-learning courses.
Well, I should go and work on my essay now.
Love Guy

Self study

Find out about the history of a school, college or university where you have studied. Make a timeline of the key events that you think are interesting. Using only the timeline, write a short text or make a brief presentation to explain the history to other students.

Lesson 2

Language study

Chen has an assignment to write about the development of information and communications technology, so he wants to record and learn words for change. He decides to organize the words according to different types of change. He makes a spidergram like the one below.

Task 1 Organizing vocabulary

1.1 Look at the transcript of George Blackstone's talk on pages 210 and 211. Find more words for Chen's spidergram and write them below. Look for verbs and nouns.

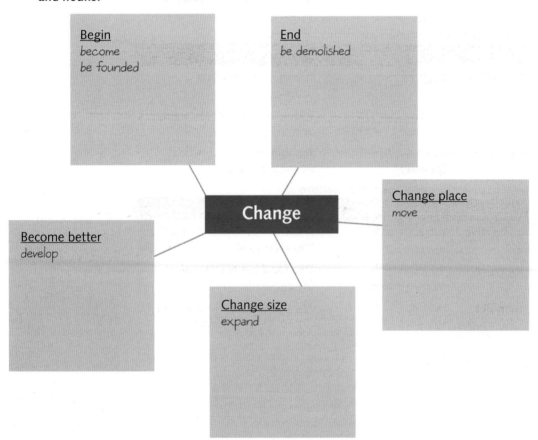

1.2 Work in groups. Add as many more verbs and nouns to each box as you can.

Chen knows that he needs to record some information about the grammar of the verbs so that he can use them correctly in his assignment.

Noticing grammar patterns

Changes in a general situation

Become is used for changes in a general situation. This verb uses the same pattern in a sentence as *be*.

pattern	example
become + adjective	*The Stevenson Institute became popular.*
become + noun phrase	*The Morgan-Stevenson College became a university (in 1967).*

Task 2 Practising grammar patterns

Has a general situation in your school, city or country changed? Write a few sentences to show these changes using the verb patterns with *become* from the box above.

Noticing grammar patterns

Verb patterns

Different types of verbs have different patterns. The dictionary uses the terms *intransitive* and *transitive* to name these patterns. Intransitive verbs have a subject but no object. Transitive verbs can have an active or a passive form. The noun phrase which is the object in the active form (*the university*) becomes the subject noun phrase in the passive form.

verb type	verb pattern	example
intransitive	subject + verb	*Important events have happened.*
transitive	subject + verb (active)+ object	*A wealthy inventor rescued <u>the university</u>.*
transitive	subject + verb (passive)	*<u>The university</u> was rescued (by a wealthy inventor).*

Some verbs for change can use all these patterns.

verb type	verb pattern	example
intransitive	subject + verb	*The university started (about 150 years ago).*
transitive	subject + verb (active)+ object	*Two local businessmen started <u>the university</u>.*
transitive	subject + verb (passive)	*<u>The university</u> was started (by two local businessmen).*

Noticing language

Word meanings

Revolution is a general noun. It is used with adjectives (*industrial*, *green*) and nouns (*information*) to label ideas about a subject. These labels summarize many ideas very concisely. People who have studied a subject know these ideas and think of them when they read or hear the label.

Movement is another general noun that can be used with adjectives (*green*) and nouns (*women's*) to label ideas.

Task 10 Using key words correctly

Below are parts of a dictionary entry for *movement*. There are four main meanings.
Choose the correct meaning for each sentence a–g. Write I, 2, 3 or 4 in each box.

1   movement (noun)
A group of people who share the same aim and work together to achieve it.
The Women's Movement campaigns for equal rights for women in society.

2   movement (noun) from ... to
The process of moving [something] from one place to another.
During the Industrial Revolution, there was a movement of people looking for work from the countryside to the cities.

3   movement (noun)
A change in the position of your body or a way of moving your body.
After the accident, the range of movement in his arm was reduced.

4   movement (noun) in
A change that leads to a new situation.
exchange rate movement; movement in the value of currency

Definitions from Macmillan Dictionary www.macmillandictionary.com

a Organizations such as Friends of the Earth are part of the environmental movement.

b Costs change as a result of price movements in materials, components and wages.

c Information is different from knowledge because it involves change and movement. You receive information and pass it to other people.

d The Trade Union movement aims to protect workers from exploitation by managers.

e When people use computers, they make small repeated movements with their hands, which can cause injury.

f The poor transport network in some developing countries makes the movement of goods from the producer to the market difficult.

g The peace movement tries to bring an end to war.

Self study

Find some words for change and development to learn. Write the word family for each word. Check in a dictionary how to say each word in the word family. Look for these words in other texts and find collocations for them. Using the words you have learnt, write some example sentences about changes you have noticed. Use the correct verb patterns and collocations.

Lesson 3
Summarizing developments

Aims
- to understand where to find summary ideas in a text
- to understand which ideas are relevant for the purpose of an essay
- to evaluate how a student has borrowed and used ideas

Guy has a job at his local supermarket, which is run as a co-operative. He is interested in finding out more about this type of business organization. He decides to choose the following essay question, from a list given by his lecturer, as it will help him to research this topic in more detail.

What factors contributed to the decline of the co-operative movement in the UK?

In order to prepare for writing his essay, Guy reads a section of his textbook, *Business organizations*.

Key words

factors
contributed to
the decline

Task 1 Reading quickly for the main idea

Below is a list of purpose statements.

1.1   **Look at the text from Guy's book on page 106. Which statement, a–g, gives the purpose of the whole chapter?**

   a to explain why the co-operative movement started

   b to explain the principles of the co-operative movement

   c to define co-operative organizations and give some examples

   d to explain how workers can participate in decisions in an organization

   e to explain the history and development of the co-operative movement

   f to explain why co-operatives have difficulty competing with supermarkets

   g to illustrate worker participation using a case study of co-operative organizations

1.2   **Which statement gives the purpose of section 7.1?**

Task 2 Reading carefully

Read the whole of section 7.1 on page 106. Match each paragraph to one of the remaining purpose statements in the list from Task 1. Write the correct number in each box above. One paragraph matches two purpose statements.

Chapter 7 Participation and Control

Both owners of organizations and workers in organizations have tried to find ways for workers to participate in the process of making decisions and to have some control over their working lives. One way is for owners to redesign tasks to make them more satisfying for workers, usually by forming work groups or teams. Another way is for the workers to become the owners of the organization. This form of participation is called a co-operative.

7.1 Co-operatives

(1) Co-operatives are organizations in which people have joined together to meet common needs and achieve common goals. They are owned by their members, who share the profits and take decisions democratically. There are many different types of co-operatives, depending on the shared needs and goals of the members. For example, consumer co-operatives are owned by customers who join together to make sure that the goods and services they want to buy are good quality and a fair price. Worker co-operatives are owned by the workers in an industry.

(2) The modern concept of co-operatives began in the north of England in 1844, when a group of workers in the town of Rochdale opened a small shop. They became known as the Rochdale Pioneers. At this time, working practices were changing as a result of the Industrial Revolution. Goods were made cheaply in factories, but workers had to move from the countryside to the cities where the factories were located. Working conditions were poor, and workers received low wages and lived in crowded communities. These new communities grew rapidly, but the number of shops did not expand to meet their needs. The local shopkeepers were able to charge high prices because people had no choice about where to buy their food. The workers in Rochdale could not afford the high prices for food in these local shops. They decided that, by working together, they could find basic food items at a lower price. Initially, the shop only sold flour, oatmeal, sugar and butter.

(3) The first co-operative was based on values of self-help, democracy, honesty and taking responsibility for other people. Their way of doing business was unusual at that time, because every customer of the shop became a member of the co-operative and so had a true stake in the business. Anyone could become a member if they bought goods at the shop. Purchases could only be made in cash and the profits were shared among the members, depending on how much money they spent in the shop.

(4) The reputation of the co-op shop was quickly established. It attracted large numbers of customers, who knew that they could buy quality products at fair prices. By 1880, the co-operative movement had spread throughout the UK, and by the end of the 19th century, membership had reached 1.7 million people in over 1,000 co-operative societies. From that small beginning in Rochdale, the co-operative expanded to become a worldwide movement.

(5) The principles of the Rochdale Pioneers in 1844 about the right way to do business are the basis for all co-operatives today. However, these same principles make it difficult for co-operatives to compete with modern supermarkets.

Dyson, J. R. (2008) *Business organizations*. London: Roadhouse Publishers.

Key words

to redesign
satisfying
common needs/goals
share the profits
take decisions
democratically
depending on
consumer
a fair price
pioneers
working practices
factories
the countryside
working conditions
low wages
grew rapidly
the local shopkeepers
to charge high prices
afford
basic food items
at a lower price
initially
values
self-help
democracy
taking responsibility
doing business
a member
had a stake in
purchases
in cash
the profits
money they spent
the reputation
established
attracted customers
spread throughout
had reached
worldwide
the principles
the basis
to compete

Task 3 Thinking critically

Before he starts to write, Guy has to analyze the question carefully to be sure that he includes relevant information in his essay.

Study Guy's essay question and answer the questions below.

What factors contributed to the decline of the co-operative movement in the UK?

a What is the general topic? Which specific aspect of the general topic should Guy discuss?

b Does this essay ask Guy to describe (e.g., a sequence of events), or to explain by giving reasons?

c Guy's writing purpose for his essay is different from the overall purpose of Chapter 7 on page 106. However, some paragraphs contain information useful for his essay. Which paragraphs could Guy use?

d What could Guy write in his introduction?

Task 4 Reviewing language for definitions and examples

4.1 Look at paragraph 1 of section 7.1, on page 106. It contains a formal definition of the term *co-operatives*. Write the elements of the formal definition in the table below.

term / concept	general	specific	more specific
co-operatives			

4.2 Paragraph 1 also contains examples which illustrate the formal definition. Complete the table below.

example	specific	more specific
consumer co-operatives		
worker co-operatives		

Lesson 5

Working together and alone

Aims

- to understand when working together is not acceptable
- to understand how topics determine the order of ideas in sentences
- to understand how to move ideas around in sentences to fit the topic

Chen is under pressure because he has three assignments due at the end of the following week. He talks to Guy about this, and they discover that Chen has the same lecturer for a module called *Developments in information and communications technology* (ICT) as Guy had for a module called *Information and communications technology for business* in his first year.

Guy finds the essay that he wrote for his module, and they compare essay titles.

Chen's essay title is:

Software applications developed considerably in the last half of the 20th century. Outline some of these developments and explain their effect on business practices.

Guy's essay title was:

Business practices changed considerably in the last half of the 20th century. Outline some of the changes and relate these to new developments in software.

Task 1 Thinking critically about titles

Compare the essay titles above, then discuss the questions below with a partner.

a How are the essay titles similar, and how are they different?

b What is the general topic for each essay? How do you know?

Guy offers to help Chen get started on his essay by writing the introduction for him. He uses the introduction he wrote for his own essay, but he changes the position of some ideas.

Task 2 Thinking critically about texts

Compare the two introductions on page 113. Look again at the essay titles above.

a Which one is Guy's original introduction?

b Which one is the introduction he has rewritten for Chen's essay?

c How do you know?

Introduction 1

Business practices have changed a great deal in the last 30 years, and this is related to new developments in computers. Managers now produce their own reports, using word processors. Accountants prepare detailed financial information with a spreadsheet application. Everyone in a company can be contacted easily by e-mail. In this essay, I will outline these changes in detail and show that they have happened because of developments in computer software.

Introduction 2

Software applications have changed a great deal in the last 30 years, and this has had a major impact on the world of business. Word processors are now used routinely by managers to produce their own reports. Spreadsheet applications are used by accountants to present detailed financial information. E-mail enables everyone in a company to contact each other easily. In this essay, I will outline the development of software applications in detail and consider their impact on business practices.

Key words

a great deal
produce reports
word processors
accountants
detailed
financial
a spreadsheet
can be contacted
by e-mail
have happened
because of
a major impact
routinely
enables

Study smart

Is this an acceptable way for Guy to help Chen with his assignment? Discuss the question with other students and give reasons for your answer.

Chen understands that Guy wants to help him, but he is not sure he can use the introduction Guy has written. He suggests they ask Maysoun what she thinks, because she has studied at university before. They find Maysoun and show her Guy's introductions.

Task 3 Listening

 CD1-25 Listen for Maysoun's view, and answer the questions below.

a Does Maysoun think this is an acceptable way for Guy to help Chen with his assignment? What reasons does she give for her view?

b Does she feel strongly about this?

Discussion

- How does Guy try to justify helping Chen with his introduction? What is Maysoun's answer to this justification? Is her answer surprising?

Chen is pleased he does not have to use Guy's introduction. However, he realizes that by comparing the sentences in Guy's two introductions, he can learn more about ordering ideas in a sentence.

Task 4 Noticing organization

Look at sentences 2–4 of the two introductions that Guy wrote on page 113. Complete the table below to show how he moved ideas to different parts of each sentence.

topic	sentence starting point	sentence middle	sentence end
business practices	*Managers*	*produce their own reports*	*using word processors.*
software applications			
	E-mail	*enables everyone in a company*	*to contact each other.*

Task 5 Thinking critically

Look at the sentence starting points in the two introductions that Guy wrote.

a What did Guy choose to put at the beginning of each sentence?

b Why did he decide to do this?

c What kinds of statements did he put at the end of his sentences? Look back to Unit 3 to help you answer this question.

Noticing grammar patterns

Organizing ideas

Ideas can be moved to different places in a sentence to fit the topic. This often requires the verb forms to change between active and passive. It may also change statements of method and purpose.

Managers	*produce*	*reports*	*using*	*word processors*	method
Reports	*are produced*	*by managers*	*using*	*word processors*	
Word processors	*are used*	*by managers*	*to produce*	*reports*	purpose

Task 6 Practising language patterns

Look at the notes a–c below. Use them to complete texts 1–6. Change the order of ideas to fit the topic for each text.

a heat / beans / gently in pan / stir / beans / with a spoon / not burn

1 Cook beans by following this simple recipe.

_____

_____

_____

Serve the beans on toast.

2 You need only a pan and a spoon to cook beans.

Use _____

_____

_____

Serve the beans on toast.

b hands / protect / lab coats / heat-resistant gloves / wear / protect clothes from chemicals

3 The laboratory is a hazardous place, so always use the safety equipment. Safety glasses are used to protect eyes.

_____

_____

_____

4 Make sure you wear protective clothing so that chemicals or flames cannot cause damage. Eyes can be protected using safety glasses.

_____

_____

_____

c Internet / quickly / find up-to-date information / library / provide / more reliable information

5 There are two main sources of information at university.

_____

_____

_____

6 Different types of information are found in different locations.

_____

_____

_____

Task 7 Writing

Help Chen to write his essay introduction. Read the essay title and Chen's first sentence, below. Tick ☑ the best option for each of the next three sentences, a–c. Make sure each sentence relates to the paragraph topic introduced in the first sentence.

Software applications developed considerably in the last half of the 20th century. Outline some of these developments and explain their effect on business practices.

First sentence: In the last half of the 20th century, there was a revolution in information and communications technology (ICT).

a 1 Designers made smaller computers with a dramatically expanded memory size. ☐

   2 Computers became smaller because their memory size expanded dramatically. ☐

   3 The size of computer memory expanded dramatically, so computers became smaller. ☐

b 1 Communication across long distances was enabled using new software applications. ☐

   2 Designers developed new software applications to enable communication across long distances. ☐

   3 New software applications were developed to enable communication across long distances. ☐

c 1 E-mail and the Internet connected people in different parts of the world. ☐

   2 People in different parts of the world were connected by e-mail and the Internet. ☐

   3 In different parts of the world, people were connected by e-mail and the Internet. ☐

Last sentence: In this essay, I will outline these developments in detail and explain their impact on business practices.

Self study

Find a text on a topic related to your subject of study. Look of the introduction to the text. Can you find a definition, some examples or some information about the development of an idea? Look at the beginnings of the sentences in each paragraph. Do the sentence starting points relate to the topic of the paragraph?

Unit 7

Something to say

Lesson 1

Joining a meeting

> ### Aims
> - to understand what is involved when speaking in a meeting
> - to practise word stress and intonation to show interest
> - to practise introductions in a meeting

Chen has to give a presentation to his class for his next assignment, but he is very worried about speaking in front of a large group of people. Even though he feels confident speaking to Guy and Maysoun, he is worried that his English is not good enough to speak about an academic topic, especially to students whose first language is English.

> ### Discussion
> - How important is it to speak about academic topics with other students at university? Why?
> - How confident would you feel discussing an academic topic in English with a group of students at university? What problems would you face? Make a list of them and keep it to review at the end of the unit. What could you do to make yourself feel more confident?

Guy thinks Chen speaks English very well. He suggests to Chen that his problem is not about language, but about speaking to people he does not know well. Guy has seen a notice asking for volunteers to join the International Students' Association Committee, and he persuades Chen to come with him to a meeting.

Task 1 Preparing to listen

Read the flier on page 118 for the International Students' Association Committee, then answer the questions below.

a What is the purpose of the committee?

b What issues do you think would concern international students studying in the UK?

c Why is it important to promote greater awareness of international students' needs?

Get involved – the International Students' Association Committee needs ▶ YOU

We aim to:

- provide a place for international students to meet informally
- support international students to discuss issues that concern them
- promote greater awareness of international students' needs on campus

The International Students' Association Committee meets each Monday evening in the students' union committee room from 5.15 to 7.15 p.m.

We are a friendly group of students from many different countries. Join us for a cup of tea or coffee and have your say about issues that concern us all.

Issue of the week: Should lecturers give feedback to students on their exams?

Key words

get involved

committee

informally

to discuss issues

concern

promote awareness

have your say

give feedback

Task 2 Thinking critically

2.1 Look again at the flier above. How will attending the committee meeting help Chen to feel more confident in speaking to his class about an academic topic?

2.2 What do you expect him to say at the meeting?

Task 3 Listening for information

3.1 ⊚CD2-1 **Listen to the start of the meeting. Match each of the committee roles a–e, below, to the activities 1–5 they are responsible for. Write the correct number in each box.**

committee role	activity
a chair ☐ _____	**1** keeping a record of the money paid to the committee and what it spends
b secretary ☐ _____	**2** making sure that the activities of the committee are advertised around the university
c treasurer ☐ _____	**3** contributing to the discussion and sharing any tasks the committee decides to do
d publicity officer ☐ _____	**4** taking the minutes (a record of the decisions and action points) of each meeting
e member ☐ _____	**5** keeping order, managing the agenda (the points to be discussed) and making sure everyone has a chance to speak

3.2 **Underneath each committee role a–e, write the name of the student who has that role on the committee.**

Task 4 Listening for speaker's purpose

Listen to the start of the discussion again. Answer the questions below.

a How did the committee members try to make Guy and Chen feel welcome?

b How did others at the meeting feel when they heard Chen was studying Computer Science? How do you know?

c What was Ibrahim's purpose when he spoke to Patti at the end?

Task 5 Noticing language

Read the transcript on pages 214 and 215, and underline the parts which helped you to complete Task 4.

Task 6 Thinking critically

6.1 **Which committee member is least confident about using English? How do you know?**

6.2 **Which students have hesitations and false starts? Do these matter?**

6.3 **How do you think Chen feels about speaking now? Why?**

Noticing language patterns

Showing interest

Intonation is the way that your voice rises and falls (goes up and down) when you speak. The students at the meeting sound really interested in Chen when they say, *Oh! Really! Hey!* This is because they use a strong rise–fall intonation.

Task 7 Practising language for showing interest

7.1 **CD2-2 Listen to the words below. Repeat them, and try to copy the intonation.**
Oh! Really! Hey!

7.2 **Work in pairs to complete the exercises below.**

Student A: Tell student B something interesting about yourself.

Student B: Show that you are interested, using one of the words above with the correct intonation.

7.3 **Change roles and repeat Exercise 7.2.**

Noticing language patterns

Syllables and word stress

English words have different numbers of syllables and different stress patterns. In each word, one syllable is stressed. This syllable sounds a little louder and higher in tone than the other syllables, e.g., *dis'**cuss***.

The stress pattern of a word stays the same in normal speech, so listeners use it to help them recognize the word. It is important to get the stress pattern of a word correct, so that people can understand you.

Lesson 3
Evaluating presentations

Aims

- to explore problems in giving presentations
- to produce a checklist to evaluate student presentations
- to learn useful word stress patterns

After attending the International Students' Association Committee meeting, Chen is feeling more confident about giving a presentation to his classmates. He has asked Guy and Maysoun to listen to him practise and give him feedback on his visuals. Maysoun has given many presentations before, both in Arabic and in English.

Discussion

- Have you ever given a presentation, in English or in your own language? How did you feel? What problems did you experience? Make a list of these problems for your group.

Task 1 Preparing to listen

The topic of Chen's presentation is *malware.*

Do you know the meaning of this word? What does Chen have to do to help listeners to understand the meaning?

Task 2 Listening critically

2.1 ⓝCD2-11 **Listen to Chen's first presentation and look at his slides, below.**

2.2 **Discuss the slides. How useful are they?**

2.3 **Make notes to give Chen feedback on how easy or difficult it is to understand his presentation.**

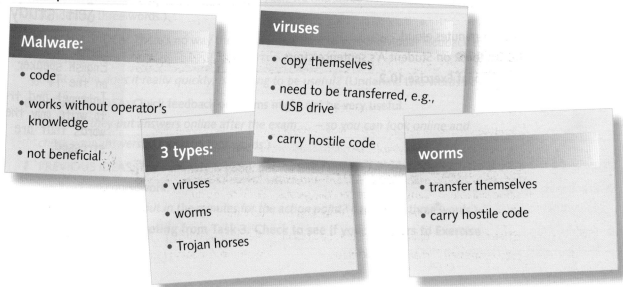

Task 3 Listening for information

 **CD2-12 Listen to Maysoun's and Guy's feedback, and answer the questions below.**

a Was Chen's presentation successful? Give your reasons.

b What did Maysoun and Guy notice that you did not?

c What suggestions do they give?

Study smart

Work in groups. Make a checklist for good presentations, using Maysoun and Guy's suggestions from Task 3. Add ideas of your own.

Task 4 Listening and note taking

4.1 **CD2-13** Look at Chen's slides on page 126. Listen to his second presentation and the feedback. Make notes on the different types of malware in a tree diagram.

4.2 What did Chen think of his second presentation?

Task 5 Thinking critically

5.1 What improvements did Chen make the second time he did his presentation? What does he still need to do?

5.2 What is more important: being academic or being interesting? Do you think memorization would help or not?

5.3 Find any false starts and hesitations in the two presentation transcripts on pages 218, 219 and 220. Do they matter?

Study smart

Add points from Task 5 to your presentations checklist.

Noticing language patterns

Word stress

CD2-14 Chen sometimes does not say technical terms clearly; he gives them incorrect stress. Listen to the words below from Chen's presentation. Repeat them using the correct stress.

Chen's incorrect stress	correct stress
'malicious	ma'licious
ope'rator	'operator

Sometimes, stress in related words stays on the same syllable. Sometimes, it moves to a different syllable. Listen to these words and repeat them.

pattern	examples in Chen's presentation	other examples
same syllable stressed	'danger, en'danger, 'dangerous, in'fect, in'fected, in'fection	po'llute, po'llution, po'llutants, po'lluter
different syllable stressed	'operate, 'operator, ope'ration, 'malware, ma'licious	'flexible, flexi'bility 'memorize, memori'zation

Noticing language patterns

Word endings and stress

⊕CD2-14 Some very frequent word endings control word stress. If you memorize them, it is easier to remember correct word stress. These word endings always move the stress to the previous syllable, even when a further word ending is added. Listen to the words below and repeat them.

word ending	examples
-ic	spe'cific, spe'cifically, eco'nomic, demo'cratic
-ity	a'bility, responsi'bility
-ion	organi'zation, inter'national
-ify	i'dentify, 'specify, 'verify
-ial	'special, 'social, fi'nancial
-ious	ma'licious, de'licious

Task 6 Practising word stress

6.1 Underline the stressed syllable in each word below.

a genetics

b expectations

c technical

d compatibility

e publicity

f exemplify

g material

h nutritious

i professionally

j verification

6.2 Practise saying these words out loud with a partner.

Study smart

Chen also says *Tro'jan horses* when he should say *Trojan 'horses*. This is a key technical term in Computer Science, so he needs to make sure he can say it with the correct stress. You have to make sure that you know correct word stress for all your technical terms. If you are not sure, use a specialist dictionary or ask an English speaker who knows your subject.

Task 7 Practising language

7.1 Look at the transcript of Chen's second presentation, on pages 219 and 220. What does Chen say to begin? How many other ways of starting a presentation can you think of?

7.2 Practise introducing a presentation to other students, using a title of your own or one that your teacher suggests. Speak loudly and clearly. Remember to get the word and sentence stress right. Other students should try to write down your title.

Self study

Prepare a short presentation (one to two minutes). In your presentation, describe how some resources are organized, or define and briefly describe a concept. See Unit 5 for help. Make a visual to show with the presentation. Check the word stress for your key words. Practise your presentation using the visual. Do not memorize the presentation. Try to get the time right (not more than two minutes).

Lesson 4
Academic discussions: revolution, movement and stress

Aims
- to practise presentations
- to practise contributing to an academic discussion

Task 1 Speaking

1.1 **Think about your presentation worries. What would you most like to improve?**

1.2 **Work in pairs to complete the exercises below.**

Student A: Without notes, practise the short presentation that you prepared as self study. Ask in advance for specific feedback.

Student B: Listen and ask the speaker about anything you don't understand. Give feedback using your evaluation checklist.

1.3 **Change roles and repeat Exercise 1.2.**

1.4 **Practise your presentation again with another student.**

Study smart

Did you improve with each practice presentation you did in Task 1?
What was most difficult? How did questions from other students help?
What will you do differently next time?

Task 2 Preparing to listen

In Unit 6, Lesson 2, you listened to Maysoun, Chen and Guy working out the meaning of a key word, *revolution*, in an academic discussion. They each made contributions and, together, they built their understanding.

Work in pairs. Together, try to remember all the types of revolution that were mentioned in the discussion that Chen, Maysoun and Guy had.

Task 3 Listening

⊙CD2-15 **Listen again to the three students working out the meaning of** *revolution*. **Answer the questions below.**

a Who makes the biggest contribution?

b Write the name of the student who makes each kind of contribution below.

  1 gives ideas

  _____

  2 asks for ideas

  _____

  3 asks for confirmation or help to refine an idea

  _____

  4 confirms someone else's idea

  _____

  5 refines someone else's idea (e.g., by adding reasons, examples, effects)

  _____

  6 shows interest in someone else's idea

  _____

c In the transcript of the discussion on pages 211 and 212, underline the words and phrases the students use to signal their contributions.

Task 4 Thinking critically

4.1 **What do you think an engineering student might say about the meaning of** *revolution*?

4.2 **What concept do all the different kinds of revolution share?**

Study smart

The concept of the Industrial Revolution is based on the idea of a turning wheel. Many technical terms are based on a meaning that is borrowed from something very simple and non-technical. This type of shared meaning is called a *metaphor*. Think of a technical term you know that is based on a metaphor. Explain it to another student.

In the next part of the lesson, you are going to participate in two discussions and evaluate your contributions each time. You will count the number of contributions that you make using something small, such as a paperclip or a matchstick. So you will need a few of these in your hand at the start of each discussion.

Study smart

You are going to discuss the word *movement* for about two minutes. Use the list of contributions from Task 3 to identify the types of contributions you would like to make to this discussion.

Task 5 Preparing to speak

Explore the different meanings of the word *movement*. Prepare by yourself.

a Look back to Unit 6, Lesson 2 for some ideas.

b Check for more meanings in your own dictionary.

c Think of some examples to explain the meanings you find.

Task 6 Speaking

6.1 Work in groups. Discuss the meaning of the word *movement*. Keep your books closed, and keep the discussion going as long as you can. Each time you make a contribution, put one of your paperclips on the table in front of you.

6.2 When the discussion is over, count the paperclips. Who made the most contributions in your group? Help each other to decide which kinds of contributions each of you made.

Study smart

Next, you are going to discuss the word *stress* for about two minutes. Use the list of contributions from Task 3 to identify the types of contributions you would like to make to this discussion.

Task 7 Preparing to speak

Explore the different meanings of the word *stress*. Prepare by yourself.

a Check for meanings in your own dictionary.

b Think of some examples to explain the meanings.

Task 8 Speaking

8.1 Work in groups. Discuss the meaning of the word *stress*. Keep your books closed, and keep the discussion going as long as you can. Each time you make a contribution, put one of your paperclips on the table in front of you.

8.2 When the discussion is over, count the paperclips. Who made the most contributions in your group? Help each other to decide which kinds of contributions each of you made.

8.3 Is there a metaphor in the meanings of *stress* that you discussed?

Self study

Find a group discussion in English to listen to on the Internet or on TV. Are there any speakers who contribute too much or too little? Try to identify the types of contribution.

Lesson 5

Discussing the challenge of speaking at university

Aims
- to listen to a discussion
- to hold a discussion
- to review a discussion

Chen has been building up his confidence to speak in academic contexts and doing lots of practice with his friends. He has received an e-mail from his former EAP teacher, Nick, who wants him to come and talk to a group of students studying on a foundation course[1]. Nick hopes that Chen will be able to tell the students what university is like.

Task 1 Thinking critically

1.1 Discuss with your teacher and your classmates whether you would like to listen to Chen's discussion before you have your discussion, or whether you would like to discuss first and then listen. Be prepared to justify your choice and persuade other students to accept it.

1.2 If you decide to have your discussion before you listen to Chen, complete Task 5 first (see page 134).

Chen's discussion

You are going to listen to Chen's discussion on university life for international students.

Study smart

Look at the lists below. They show the types of contribution made by speakers in a discussion. Discussions often have a leader with a role similar to a chair at a meeting. Nick is the leader of the discussion you will hear, helped by Chen. They have to lead the discussion, i.e., to make the meeting flow smoothly (see the left-hand list below). They can also make the same contributions as the other speakers (see the right-hand list).

Discussion leader(s)
- start the discussion
- ask people to contribute
- keep the contributions relevant
- summarize ideas

Speakers
- give ideas
- ask for ideas
- ask for confirmation or help to refine an idea
- confirm someone else's idea
- refine someone else's idea (e.g., by adding reasons, examples, effects)
- show interest in someone else's idea

[1] Many universities offer one-year *foundation* courses of EAP and academic studies, to prepare students for their degree studies. The academic studies are useful in widening students' general knowledge (e.g., international issues) and skills, such as IT.

Task 2 Listening

⊙CD2-16 Listen to the discussion and answer the questions below.

a Which types of contribution from the lists on page 132 does Nick make?

b How does Chen help Nick?

c What specific ideas does Nick contribute?

Task 3 Listening for ideas

Study the list of ideas below, which were contributed in the discussion. Listen to the discussion again and number the ideas in the correct sequence. The first one has been done for you.

a It's difficult for Chen to give presentations and discuss topics in class. ☐ 1

b It's important to contribute – don't worry about making mistakes. ☐

c Teachers have important information and young people don't want to waste class time on their own personal opinions. ☐

d When the topic is important, you can have ideas, but it's difficult and takes time to prepare them in English. ☐

e Group harmony is important, and so challenge and argument feels wrong. ☐

f In Iran, high-school students are expected to listen quietly to the teacher, too. ☐

g If you don't speak, people will think you are not interested or you don't understand. ☐

h High-school students in China and Thailand are expected by their teachers to stay quiet and listen. ☐

i Some high-school students feel that they need permission from the teacher to speak. ☐

j Students from many countries are afraid of losing face if they make mistakes. ☐

Task 4 Listening and reading for contributions

Listen to the discussion again, and read the transcript on pages 221–224. Find examples of each type of contribution below. Write the contributions and the names of the speakers who make them.

a gives ideas

_____

b asks for ideas

_____

c asks for confirmation or help to refine an idea

_____

d confirms someone else's idea

_____

e refines someone else's idea (e.g., by adding reasons, examples, effects)

_____

f shows interest in someone else's idea

_____

Class discussion

You are going to discuss the following question:
Why do some students stay quiet in discussions?

Study smart

Prepare for the discussion by thinking of some reasons why students don't want to speak in discussions.

Task 5 Discussing

Work in groups of six to eight students. Complete the exercises below.

a Decide which person will take the role of discussion leader. Decide whether you want someone to take notes. If possible, record your discussion so you can listen again and evaluate your participation.

b After your discussion, write down some answers to the discussion question. Share your ideas with the other groups in your class.

c If you decided to have your discussion before you listened to Chen, complete tasks 2, 3 and 4 next.

Evaluation

You are now going to evaluate the two discussions from this lesson.

Task 6 Thinking critically

6.1 Compare your group's performance with Nick's group's performance. Answer the questions below.

a Did everyone in your group have a chance to speak?

b Did you find and record some answers to the discussion question?

c Look at the kinds of contributions listed in the Study smart box on page 132. Write the names of the people in your group who made each of these contributions.

6.2 Compare your own performance with Nick's group. Answer the questions below.

a How much did you contribute?

b What do you think you did well?

c What do you think you need to improve?

d How will you change next time?

Self study

Think about the challenges you face in writing at university. Bring some notes to the next lesson for discussion.

Lesson 1

Reasons and results

Aims
- to make notes on reasons and results
- to understand language patterns for links between sentences
- to use key language for linking reasons and results

It's November, and several weeks of the first semester at Gateway University have passed. Most students are more confident now with new ideas and new concepts, but some students have other worries.

Task 1 Reading quickly for the main idea

Look at the text below. It explains what the students are doing at this stage of the semester. Tick ✓ the phrase a–e that best summarizes their main activity.

a doing difficult assignments

b talking to lecturers

c meeting each other

d using feedback to improve assignments

e preparing for degree studies

Mid-semester at Gateway University

By mid-semester, students are working hard on their assignments. Some first drafts have been completed, and lecturers are giving feedback to students, who are taking the opportunity to improve their earlier drafts. Chen feels happy because his current assignment is mostly programming, so he has to write only a little English. Also, he has received some good feedback from his lecturer and he has met a new friend, Xiaohua. Xiaohua has just joined the foundation year course at Gateway University to prepare for starting a degree in Computer Science next year. Because she joined the course late, Xiaohua missed some writing classes. As a result, she is having problems with writing academic texts. She is worried, so she asks Chen to help her to understand some feedback from her subject lecturer for International Issues, Martin Gibson.

> **Key words**
>
> taking the opportunity
>
> current
>
> only a little
>
> as a result
>
> having problems with
>
> International Issues

Task 2 Reading carefully for detail

Read the text above again, and answer the questions below.

a How does Chen feel? Why?

b How does Xiaohua feel? Why?

Task 3 Reading carefully to make notes

The two flow diagrams below show how the students' feelings are linked to the reasons for these feelings.

Which flow diagram represents which student? Write the missing names and the missing reasons in the appropriate boxes.

Study smart

The links between reasons (or causes) and results (or effects), like the links between the stages in a process, can be shown clearly in note form using flow diagrams. The arrows point from the reason to the result. The flow diagram shows that Xiaohua's worries began with just one reason: she arrived late. This started a chain of results leading to her current worries, each result becoming a reason for the next result. In contrast, Chen has three different reasons why he is happy.

Task 4 Reading carefully to identify reasons and results

Look at the sentences below describing reasons and results. Underline the reasons and circle the results. The first sentence has been done for you.

a Chen feels happy because <u>his current assignment is mostly programming</u>.

b His current assignment is mostly programming, so he has to write only a little English.

c Because she joined the course late, Xiaohua missed some writing classes.

d As a result, she is having problems with writing academic texts.

e She is worried, so she asks Chen to help her to understand some feedback from her subject lecturer.

Noticing grammar patterns

Linking reasons and results or causes and effects

There are two main ways to link reasons and results between sentences:

1 Use a linking word.

2 Use a signpost word.

1 Two sentences can be joined together using linking words.

linking pattern	example
result + *because* + reason	*Chen feels happy because his current assignment is mostly programming …*
reason + *so* + result	*… his current assignment is mostly programming, so he has to write only a little English*

2 Sometimes the sentences are not joined together, but there is a signpost word at the start of the first or second sentence to point the way to the following reason or result.

linking pattern	example
reason (sentence 1). *As a result*, + result (sentence 2)	*Xiaohua missed some writing classes. As a result, she is having problems with writing academic texts.*

It is important not to confuse linking words and signpost words. Linking words can join sentences together, but signpost words can only point the way to the idea in the second sentence.

Task 5 Noticing grammar patterns: reasons and results

Look again at the text on page 135, and complete the exercises below.

a Find more words in the text that helped you to complete the flow diagrams from Task 3.

b Write the linking words in the left-hand column of the table below.

c Write the signpost words in the right-hand column.

linking words	signpost words

Task 6 Practising grammar patterns: reasons and results

Are you happy or worried about your studies at the moment? Explain why. Say or write your answer using the linking words and patterns that you found in Task 5.

Chen wants to make Xiaohua happy. He shows her a poster for the English Conversation Club. It's Friday, the end of the week. They decide to look at her essay on Saturday, when they have more time, and to go to the quiz tonight.

International Students
What do you know?
It's quiz night tonight!
Come along to the English Conversation Club.

! Improve your English and win a prize at the same time!

Task 7 Listening for reasons and results

Prepare for the quiz as your teacher suggests. Close your books and work in teams to do the conversation club quiz.

Task 8 Noticing language for reasons and results

Look at the quiz questions below. The question word *Why?*, in questions 1 and 7, asks for reasons. Find more examples of key language for reasons or results in the quiz questions. Underline the examples you find.

1 Why was the university founded?

2 What was the reason for choosing the university's first name, the Stevenson Institute?

3 What was the result of the campaign by Jenny Ellis?

4 What caused overcrowding at the Stevenson Institute in 1880?

5 What were the two main factors that contributed to the institute's financial difficulties during rebuilding?

6 What made Mr Morgan, a wealthy inventor, grateful to the institute?

7 Why was the name changed to the Morgan-Stevenson College?

8 What did the change to university status in 1967 mean for the students?

9 What is the reason for the gateway in the university logo?

10 What has led to the main expansion in Gateway University student numbers since the 1960s?

Noticing grammar patterns

Linking reasons and results or causes and effects using *make*

The verb *make* is used to link reasons to results using adjectives.

linking pattern	examples
reason (noun phrase) + *make* + result (noun phrase + adjective)	*The quiz makes Chen very happy.* *The feedback makes Xiaohua worried.*

Task 9 Practising grammar patterns

Use suitable adjectives from the box to complete the sentences below, taken from earlier units.

> persuasive   unstable   efficient   safer   flexible   visible   clearer
>
> specific   confident   bug-free

a Positive feedback makes students more ___confident___.

b Online learning makes study more ___flexible___.

c Each programmer's purpose is to make the program ___efficient___, adaptable and ___bug free___.

d Pollutants make ecological systems in the environment ___unstable___.

e Adding examples helps to make ideas ___clearer___.

f Adjusting the Bunsen burner air hole makes the flame ___visible___.

g In the Dewey Decimal system, we can add a decimal point and more numbers to make the topics more ___specific___.

h Give reasons to make your claim more ___persuasive___.

i These rules help to make the lab ___safer___.

Task 10 Writing

Write a paragraph about the reasons for feedback on writing. Write 100 to 150 words. Use the language patterns for reasons and results that you have studied in this lesson.

Self study

Think about how your language links reasons and results. Are there any similarities and differences compared with English?

Lesson 2
Risks and hazards

Aims
- to understand the idea of risk assessment
- to analyze and use language patterns for levels of probability
- to understand grammar patterns for links between noun phrases

It's November. Maysoun is going on a weekend field trip in the countryside. The students are staying in a youth hostel. They will be doing fieldwork outside and analyzing their results. Before they leave Summerford, they meet Dr Charles in the lab to check their equipment and complete risk assessment forms.

Key words

field trip
fieldwork
youth hostel
equipment
risk assessment

Discussion
- What are the possible dangers or hazards of doing fieldwork in the UK countryside in November?

Task 1 Preparing to listen

Assess the probability level of the hazards in the left-hand column of the risk assessment form below. Write *high, medium, low* or *zero* in the right-hand column.

hazards	probability level
a trips and falls	
b cuts and scratches	
c cold	
d heat	
e poisonous spiders or snakes	
f serious diseases	
g road traffic accidents	
h attacks by wild animals	
i insect bites	

Task 2 Listening

⊙CD2-17 **Listen to Dr Charles' talk. Check your answers to Task 1 using the information she gives.**

Task 3 Thinking critically

3.1 **How would you describe Dr Charles' attitude to the students in the class? Choose one of the following and give reasons for your answer.**

   a She is angry about their interruptions.

   b She is worried that they can't take responsibility for their own safety.

   c She is going to make sure they do the fieldwork properly.

3.2 **What expressions does Dr Charles use to emphasize important points?**

Task 4 Noticing language

Dr Charles uses a wide range of language to show different levels of probability. For example, *may, can, low probability, always*.

Find some more examples of this language in the transcript on pages 223 and 224.

Task 5 Analyzing language patterns

The table below shows the three main language patterns used for levels of probability.

5.1 **Write the key language from Task 4 in the appropriate places in the table. The four examples given in Task 4 have been done for you.**

level of probability	verb	probability	frequency/number
high			always
medium	may, can		
low		low probability	
none / zero			

5.2 **Add the words below to the table in the appropriate place.**

might   could   none   certain   few   most   some
often   rarely   sometimes   never

Study smart

Students sometimes use the word *should* incorrectly. Remember that the word *should* is generally not used for probability. It is usually an instruction word – it tells people what to do or gives advice:
There should be a bottle of disinfectant on every bench.

Task 6 Practising language patterns for probability

6.1 **Complete the sentences below in a suitable way, using key language for probability.**

a The weather in the UK _____.

b The weather in my country _____.

c In the UK, wild animals _____.

d Ticks _____.

e Feedback on writing assignments _____.

f Learning English on a computer _____.

g Students who take responsibility for their learning _____.

h Teachers who want to help their students _____.

6.2 **Underline the key language for probability that you used. Compare your ideas with another student.**

Task 6 Practising language patterns: familiar to new

The sentences a–g, below, form a complete paragraph. Tick ✓ the appropriate sentence (1 or 2) in b, e and g so the ideas link clearly from familiar to new.

a The risk of becoming infected with Lyme disease is not high, because only a few ticks carry the bacteria.

b 1 Also, it is only at the end of a blood feed that the bacteria spread from the tick into the bite.

   2 Also, the bacteria do not spread from the tick into the bite until the end of a blood feed.

c This delay means that infection can be avoided if the tick is removed early.

d If the tick is not detected early, it might infect the bite.

e 1 The bite then develops a characteristic circular, spreading rash.

   2 A characteristic circular, spreading rash is then developed round the bite.

f Once you see this symptom, more serious symptoms such as heart problems may develop.

g 1 To avoid any serious effects, it is important to be treated quickly with antibiotics.

   2 It is important to be treated quickly with antibiotics to avoid any serious effects.

Noticing language patterns

Familiar information

Ideas can be linked between sentences in a paragraph using the familiar to new pattern. The new information at the end of one sentence can be repackaged as familiar information at the beginning of the next sentence. The repackaged information is in a shorter, summarized form. It is often a pronoun, e.g., *they*. It can also be a noun phrase that repeats a noun from the previous sentence or summarizes information using a general noun.

Task 7 Noticing grammar patterns: repackaging information

7.1 Complete the topic noun phrases below without looking back at the text in Task 6.

topic noun phrase	new information (familiar info)
a The risk of becoming infected with Lyme disease	is not high, because only a few ticks carry the bacteria.
b (Also) the _____	do not spread from the tick into the bite until the end of a blood feed.
c This _____	means that infection can be avoided if the tick is removed early.
d (If) the _____	is not detected early, it might infect the bite.
e The _____	then develops a characteristic circular, spreading rash.
f (Once you see) this _____,	more serious symptoms such as heart problems may develop.
g (To avoid) any serious _____,	it is important to be treated quickly.

7.2 Which sentences start with an idea that was introduced in the previous sentence?

7.3 Underline the words that link the new and familiar information. Which are repeated nouns, and which are general nouns that summarize information?

Noticing grammar patterns

Linking ideas

How you choose to begin a sentence depends on what is familiar and what is new information for your reader. This affects the choice of linking language which follows.

example	type of link	choice
Ticks *cause* Lyme disease. Lyme disease *is caused by* ticks.	verb (*cause*)	active or passive
Feedback *results in* better writing. Better writing *results from* feedback.	verb (*results*)	preposition *in* or *from*
Xiaohua is worried *because* she arrived late. She arrived late, *so* she is worried. *Because* she arrived late, she is worried.	linking word (*because/so*)	choice of linking word *because* or *so* or position of *because*

Task 8 Practising grammar patterns for linking ideas

Look at the text below about risk assessment. Choose suitable linking language to complete the gaps.

Maysoun is not worried about poisonous snakes and spiders (a) _____

Dr Charles says that there are no really dangerous wild animals in the UK. However, she is worried about ticks (b)_____ they can (c) _____ Lyme disease,

(d) _____ she looks for information on the Internet. Her Internet research

(e) _____ a lot of interest from the other students (f) _____ their worries about Lyme disease.

Task 9 Writing a paragraph

Write a short paragraph about hazards in the countryside in your country. The first sentence should be general. The following sentences should become more and more specific. They should start with familiar information.

Study smart

Review your text from Task 9. Think about the questions below.
- Did you use any cause–effect links?
- What kinds of links did you make from one sentence to the next between new and familiar information?
- Did you repackage information using noun phrases?
- Did you use repeated nouns or general nouns to summarize ideas?

Exchange texts with a partner and discuss the linking between the ideas.

Self study

Read Xiaohua's essay on pages 148 and 149 with the comments that her lecturer has written. Make notes to answer the questions below.

Do you think Xiaohua understands the links between causes and effects that she is writing about? What are the main problems in her essay? Find examples from her text to support your view. Are there any good points about Xiaohua's draft?

Lesson 4

A high school essay

Aims
- to understand differences in school and university writing
- to evaluate a text for content, organization and language
- to use feedback to redraft a student text

On Saturday morning, Chen and Xiaohua start reviewing Xiaohua's essay, below. First, Chen reads the essay and the comments from the International Issues lecturer, Martin Gibson. Chen discusses the comments with Xiaohua.

Essay title? Check assignment ——→ The Greenhouse Effect

In school, we been taught a bit about greenhouse

Which causes which? ——————→ effect, which is because global warming. In my opinion, it is a serious way to make global warming, therefore the world become hotter and starting

Your links are not ———————→ with greenhouse effect which effects by CO_2.
clear here. Furthermore, CO_2 because of industrial using coal and oil and that because of people everywhere want to develop a high life standard nowadays.

So how is greenhouse warming? First smoke comes from fossil fuels like coal and oil and this is the C in CO_2 which goes up in the atmosphere and stops energy from the sun to get out, after first energy

No! The temperature increase ——→ from the sun getting in so energy trapped result
results from the trapped from temperature goes up. Coal is plenty in China
energy! There are many coal- because many coal power stations in my country.
fired power stations in China Maybe China is big CO_2 pollution. But China needs
because coal is plentiful! develop with India too.

The next thing which is what happens to follow from greenhouse warming is sea rise. Ice melts at polar and some small islands get drowned that results more

Again, your links are ————→ water in ocean and therefore flooding. Some people
not clear here. say that more water should be result more serious typhoon or hurricane. Moreover, it is dangerous for human beings.

There is more desert because greenhouse worming. By this rain clouds move to another place because winds changing. There is no rain because people and their animals can't live there which moves to another place

What causes what? ——————→ and eat all the grass so more desert and sandstorms in the cities like Beijing. Some other ways that greenhouse warming is making some diseases to spread.

Key words

global warming
in my opinion
smoke
fossil fuels
CO_2
trapped
coal-fired power stations
plentiful
polar
islands
drowned
flooding
typhoon
hurricane
desert
sandstorms

> You don't really answer the question. Look again at what you have to do for this assignment.
>
> You seem to be confusing cause and effect, can you make it clearer? Martin

> In conclusion, global is getting hotter and mainly because CO₂ which is from the greenhouse affect by energy for industry development. Governments should stop to make energy from coal and oil. They should use wind and sun instead and other renewable energy. That will make the world very beautiful for the people where good air to breathe.

Task 1 Listening for ideas

1.1 Look at the questions below. Which ones can you answer before listening?

a Look at the ideas about university assignments below. Which are Chen's ideas (C) and which are Xiaohua's (X)? Write C or X in each box.

1 You have to write everything you know about the topic in the assignment.

2 You have to answer the specific question in the assignment.

3 High school essays are different from university assignments.

4 University assignments are too difficult for Xiaohua.

b What does Chen say to make Xiaohua feel happier?

1.2 ⊙CD2-18 Listen to the first part of Chen and Xiaohua's conversation and check your answers.

Task 2 Listening for detail

Feedback on writing in EAP classes is usually divided into three important aspects: content, organization and language. Chen's English teacher, Nick, gave Chen a handout on his pre-sessional course to show how he would mark essays.

⊙CD2-19 Listen to the second part of Chen and Xiaohua's conversation about types of feedback. Complete the gaps in Handout 1, below.

Handout 1: EAP feedback on writing

feedback type	aspect of writing	useful questions
Content	the content (ideas) of the writing in terms of the assignment or task	Does the writer: • answer the question and follow the task (a) _____ properly? (task achievement) • include relevant and important (b) _____? • understand what the (c) _____ needs, i.e., what is familiar and what is new – what needs to be explained and what doesn't?
Organization	the way the ideas are (d) _____ in sentences and paragraphs	Do paragraphs: • maintain or develop topics clearly? • move the reader from (e) _____ to (f) _____ information? Do sentences start with (g) _____ information and then add (h) _____ information?
Language	the use of academic English	Does the writer: • use suitable academic English? • use a range of key words and language patterns for the functions, e.g., (i) _____ and effect? • link (j) _____ in the text clearly using pronouns, repeated nouns and general nouns?

Task 3 Analyzing feedback

Look at the feedback you prepared for Xiaohua. Classify your feedback into comments on content, organization and language. Use the feedback handout on page 149 to help you.

Task 4 Understanding assignment tasks: task achievement

Xiaohua's assignment is: *Write a 500-word essay to explain to one of your classmates the link between the Industrial Revolution, global climate change and developing economies.*

Answer the questions below.

a What is the general topic of Xiaohua's assignment?

b What is the specific information that the assignment asks for?

c Who is the information for? Why does Xiaohua need to think about this?

Study smart

At university, assignments are graded mainly on the ideas that the assignment asks for, and not on the language. Always read assignment tasks carefully. As well as the general topic, look for the specific aspects that you need to write about. Think about who will read it, and what is familiar/new information for them.

Task 5 Writing feedback

5.1 Work in groups. Look again at Xiaohua's draft on pages 148 and 149 and write feedback for her under the three headings *content, organization* and *language*. Say what is good. Explain what she needs to change by writing: *You need to ...*

5.2 Review with your teacher.

Task 6 Making notes in a cause–effect flow diagram

Chen was careful not to tell Xiaohua what to write. He asked her some questions and they drew cause–effect flow diagrams to help her to make her ideas clearer. The flow diagram below shows the main ideas for the first paragraph of Xiaohua's essay.

Look at the original and new drafts of Xiaohua's first and last paragraphs on page 151, and complete the exercises below.

a Try to complete the flow diagram, first from the original draft first paragraph, and then from the new draft first paragraph.

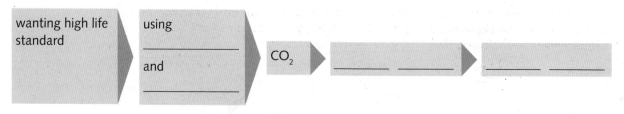

b Which draft is easier to follow and why?

Xiaohua's original draft

The Greenhouse Effect

In school, we been taught a bit about greenhouse effect, which is because global warming. In my opinion, it is a serious way to make global warming, therefore the world become hotter and starting with greenhouse effect which effects by CO_2. Furthermore, CO_2 because of industrial using coal and oil and that because of people everywhere want to develop a high life standard nowadays.

Xiaohua's new draft

The link between the Industrial Revolution, global climate change and developing economies

The Industrial Revolution was a major change in technology in Europe around 200 years ago. This change brought machines and efficient production. As a result, European economies grew. The expansion needed energy from burning large amounts of coal and oil. Burning these fuels produces CO_2, a gas which contributes to global climate change by the greenhouse effect. Global climate change has serious impacts which affect every country in the world. This essay will first explain how the greenhouse effect makes the climate warmer, and then it will examine some of the effects of this change in our climate, including the impacts on developing countries.

Last paragraph

Xiaohua's original draft

In conclusion, global is getting hotter and mainly because CO_2 which is from the greenhouse affect by energy for industry development. Governments should stop to make energy from coal and oil. They should use wind and sun instead and other renewable energy. That will make the world very beautiful for the people where good air to breathe.

Xiaohua's new draft

In conclusion, industrial development uses coal and oil. This is making the world warmer as a result of CO_2 production and the greenhouse effect. It is important to develop alternative sources of energy that will not have this effect on the climate, but this technology is not very advanced yet. Although many developing countries will be badly affected by climate change, some, for example India and China, need energy for their development. It is difficult for these countries to reduce CO_2 production without slowing their economic development.

Noticing language

Key features of academic writing

In Unit 1, you learnt about formal words in academic writing (language).

In Unit 4, you learnt that academic writing is mainly about ideas and not people (content), and often has longer noun phrases containing more ideas than other writing (language and organization).

Task 7 Analyzing academic writing

Look again at page 151. Compare Xiaohua's new first and last paragraphs with her first draft, and answer the questions below.

a What differences are there in terms of ideas, including references to people and task achievement?

b What differences are there in organization from general to specific? How is the organization better in the new draft?

c Which draft has longer sentences?

d Which draft has longer noun phrases?

e Which draft has more general nouns?

f What differences are there in cause–effect language patterns?

Study smart

Do you need to make similar changes to the ones Xiaohua made to improve your academic writing? Which changes are important for you?

Task 8 Writing: redrafting

Look back to Xiaohua's complete first draft on pages 148 and 149. Redraft one of the middle paragraphs for her by completing the exercises below.

a Make notes on the cause–effect links from the paragraph using a flow diagram.

b Use one of the new first sentences below to help you to redraft the paragraph in about 100 words. Keep Xiaohua's original ideas, but expand her examples. Remember that the paragraphs should fit with the new first and last paragraphs on page 151.

Paragraph 2

The greenhouse effect is a very important factor in global warming.

Paragraph 3

Global climate change is having serious impacts on global water systems.

Paragraph 4

Global climate change is also having serious impacts on the land.

Task 9 Writing

Write a short answer to the question *What is the link between pollution, health and economic development?* Write about 300 words for another student to read.

> **Self study**
>
> Read Guy's essay on the co-operative movement on pages 154 and 155. Make notes on the factors that contributed to the movement's decline in the 20th century. Use cause–effect flow diagrams like the ones you saw in Lessons 1 and 4.

Lesson 5

A university assignment

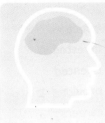

Aims

- to evaluate a university assignment
- to understand feedback on a university assignment
- to write a text linking causes and effects from notes

Guy has worked hard on a draft text for his assignment about the co-operative movement. He e-mails the draft to Dr Malik for feedback at his next tutorial.

Task 1 Understanding text organization

Look at Guy's draft assignment on pages 154 and 155. Number the paragraphs 1–7, then answer the questions below.

a Paragraphs 1 and 2 form an introduction to the assignment. What kind of information is in this introduction?

b Highlight the most general information in paragraphs 3–7.

c Compare and discuss your answers with other students.

d Compare and discuss your self study notes with other students.

Study smart

Well-organized texts are designed to be easy to read. If you find the introduction and then the most general information in each paragraph, you can quickly see the main idea and how it develops. Although you may not understand all the specific detail, you have a structure or an outline for your notes and for your understanding of the text.

Task 2 Thinking critically

Evaluate Guy's assignment in terms of task achievement, organization and language. Answer the questions below.

a Do you think Guy's assignment will get a very good grade (A), a good grade (B) or a pass grade (C)? Give your reasons.

b What do you like in Guy's text?

c What can you learn from Guy's text to improve your academic writing?

Task 5 Reading carefully

Read the text on page 159 again. Decide whether the statements below are true (T) or false (F). Write T or F in each box.

a Gateway University aims to become an international university. ☐

b According to Roy Williams, Gateway University does not recruit enough overseas students. ☐

c Income from European Union students (including UK students) is about the same as income from overseas students. ☐

d The university does not need the money from fees that overseas students pay. ☐

e Management courses are slightly more popular in 2010 than they were in 2008. ☐

f The university attracts a large number of applicants for degrees in Life Sciences. ☐

g The purpose of the report is to persuade the university managers to recruit more overseas students. ☐

Task 6 Thinking critically about data

How can small numbers of overseas students contribute such a large amount of student fees?

Noticing language patterns

Persuasive organization

When he reports the data in his proposal, Roy Williams makes three different moves.

move	example
1. He makes claims, i.e., general statements about what he thinks the figures show.	*Overseas students provide the largest source of direct income from fees.*
2. He describes some of the data in the figures, in order to support his claims.	*In 2010, the university received over 17 million pounds from overseas student fees.*
3. He interprets the data, i.e., says what he thinks it means, by drawing conclusions or trying to explain reasons.	*Increasing the number of overseas students would benefit the university financially.*

Moves in a text are like moves in a game. They are intended to achieve the overall purpose of the text. These moves are usually made in the order shown above. They are designed to persuade a reader to accept Roy Williams' claims about the data. Sometimes the moves are in separate sentences, but sometimes one sentence contains more than one move.

Example:

The number of applications for management courses has remained stable, [claim] *at just over 200 applicants* [support].

Task 7 Understanding persuasive organization

Look at paragraphs 2 and 4 of the text on page 159. Find and highlight more examples of the three moves from the box on page 160.

Task 8 Thinking critically about sources of information

Look at the text on page 159 again. The information for the sentences which interpret the data is not given in the figures or the table. Where does this information come from?

Task 9 Practising persuasive organization

Roy Williams' proposal only included data about student recruitment, but the annual report also contained a paragraph about income from teaching activities.

9.1   Study the data on page 157 again, and put the sentences below in the correct order to make a logical paragraph.

   a   Overseas students provided over 17 million pounds, compared with only
       6.5 million pounds from UK students and less than 3 million pounds from
       other EU students.

   b   This means that a relatively small number of overseas students can contribute
       a large amount of income to the university.

   c   Gateway University receives teaching income from two different sources:
       government grants and student fees.

   d   Most of the fee income is from overseas students, who make up less than
       a fifth of the student population.

   e   In 2010, teaching grants provided 22 million pounds, whereas direct income
       from student fees amounted to 26.5 million pounds.

9.2   Which move does each sentence make: claim (C), support (S) or interpretation
      (I)? Write C, S or I in each box above.

Task 10 Thinking critically about data presentation

In the paragraph from Task 9, the data from Figure 2 is not reported exactly as shown in the figure.

Look again at Figure 2, on page 157, and at the paragraph above. Answer the questions below.

a   How has the writer changed the data?

b   Why has she made these changes?

Self study

Look on the Internet or in textbooks to find other kinds of data presentation. Can you find a text which makes claims about the data and supports these claims by selecting data to describe? Try to identify the three moves in the text.

Lesson 2

Language study

Aims

- to understand language patterns for reporting data
- to understand how writers can show their viewpoint
- to write a simple report for a table of data

The language of the proposal from Lesson 1, on page 159, is impersonal. Roy Williams does not give his opinions directly. He knows that his argument will be more persuasive if the proposal and the figures speak for themselves. His academic audience values arguments based on data, not arguments based on personal stories.

Noticing grammar patterns

Labelling data and making claims

The first sentence of a proposal/report sometimes introduces the report or a figure, and says what it is about.

pattern	examples
The report <u>examines</u> + noun phrase	This report examines some of the trends … and proposes future targets.
The figure <u>shows</u> + noun phrase	Figure 1 shows student applications by region in 2010. Figure 1 shows the percentages of students who applied to Gateway University from different regions in 2010.

The noun phrase that labels data in a report can be the short title of the figure or table. However, writers usually expand these titles in their report to be clear about what the figures show.

title	student	applications	by region in 2010
expansion	the percentages of students	who applied to Gateway University	from different regions in 2010

The first sentence of a report can also present claims.

pattern	example
The figure <u>shows</u> <u>that</u> + claim	Figure 1 shows that almost one-half of Gateway University students come from outside the UK.

Task 1 Practising grammar patterns for data and claims

1.1 **For each of the short titles below, make a sentence which explains exactly what the figure shows. Use the sentence starting points below each title. Make sure you write long noun phrases to label the data accurately.**

a Figure 2: Sources of income in 2010

Figure 2 compares the amount of _____

_____

b Table 1: Courses applied for by overseas students

Table 1 shows the trends in _____

_____

1.2 **Look back to the report on page 159. Rewrite each of the sentences you wrote in Exercise 1.1 to show Roy Williams' main claim.**

a Figure 2 shows that _____

_____

b Table 1 shows that _____

_____

1.3 **Study the data on page 157 again, and write another claim for each figure.**

a Figure 2 shows that _____

_____

b Table 1 shows that _____

_____

Noticing grammar patterns

Reporting trends

Trends look back over the past from the present. Table 1, on page 157, uses data for three different years to show how numbers of applications have changed. The change can be described using verbs or nouns.

patterns with verb		examples
no change	verb + adjective	*The number of applications has remained stable.*
increase decrease }	verb + adverb	*The number of applications has risen significantly.* *The number of applications has fallen sharply.*

patterns with noun		examples
increase decrease }	adjective + noun	*There has been a significant rise in the number of applications.* *There has been a sharp fall in the number of applications.*

For general trends with no specific time, the verb form is usually the present perfect. For trends which specify the beginning and end of a period in the past, the verb form is the simple past.

Example:
The number of applications for management courses has remained stable.
From 2008 to 2009, the number of applications for management courses remained stable.

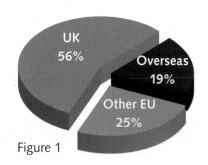

Figure 1

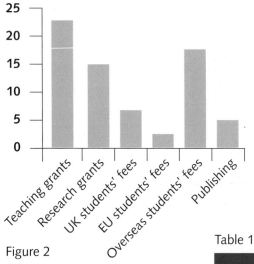

Figure 2

Table 1

	2008	2009	2010
Computer Science	250	270	320
Physical Sciences	150	90	25
Management	200	220	210
Hospitality and Tourism	90	70	50
Life Sciences	10	25	50

Task 2 Practising language patterns for reporting trends

Above are the figures and table you saw in Lesson 1. Study Table 1.

Complete the sentences below to describe trends in the data.

a _____ for Computer Science _____
significantly.

b There has been _____ in _____
for degrees in Life Sciences.

c _____ for Hospitality and Tourism_____
sharply.

d There has been _____ in _____
for degrees in Physical Sciences.

e _____ for Management _____
stable.

f Gateway University has a _____ reputation in environmental
management research.

Noticing grammar patterns

Supporting claims

Data from figures and tables can be used to support claims. This data can be described in two ways: as a separate sentence, or in a prepositional phrase added to the claim.

sentence	[claim] + prepositional phrase
In 2010, the university received over 17 million pounds from overseas student fees.	*[Application numbers have remained stable,] at just over 200 applicants.*
	[Application numbers have risen significantly,] to more than 300.
	[There has been a sharp increase in the number of applications,] with five times as many applications in 2010 as in 2008.

Task 3 Practising grammar patterns for supporting claims

Study the figures and table on page 164, and add support to the claims below. Add another sentence, or add a prepositional phrase to the first sentence.

a The largest group of students at Gateway University comes from the UK _____

_____

_____.

b Research grants provide a significant source of income for Gateway University _____

_____

_____.

c The number of students who apply for degrees in Physical Sciences has fallen _____

_____

_____.

d Degrees in Hospitality and Tourism have become much less popular _____

_____

_____.

e Computer Science is the most popular degree subject _____

_____

_____.

f The number of applications for Hospitality and Tourism and Life Sciences were the same in 2010 _____

_____

_____.

Lesson 3

Comparisons in data

Aims
- to understand claims in spoken arguments
- to use data as evidence to decide which claims are true
- to participate in a discussion using data to support and interpret claims

Guy is interested in travelling when he finishes his degree, and plans to study Chinese next year. Guy and Chen meet regularly so Guy can learn about the Chinese language and Chen can get help with English. This week, they have started a friendly argument about which language is dominant on the Internet.

Task 1 Preparing to listen

1.1 **Which language do you usually use on the Internet? How many people use the Internet in your language?**

1.2 **Which language is dominant on the Internet now? Do you think this will change?**

Task 2 Listening

2.1 **Match each claim and counterclaim below. Write the correct number in each box.**

2.2 **⊙CD2-21 Listen to Guy and Chen's conversation and answer the questions below.**

a Which is the dominant language on the Internet, according to Guy and Chen?

b What claims does each student make about his own language?

c Which student makes each claim? Write the correct name on each line.

a English is the global language.
_____

1 Maybe Chinese people use English online.

b The Internet started with English, so it's probably still the main language.
_____

2 That doesn't mean it's the main language on the Internet.

c A lot more people in China can now access the Internet.
_____

3 Lots of people speak English too, as a first, official or foreign language.

d There are lots of websites in Chinese now and lots of people in China.
_____

4 Other languages, like Chinese, are becoming more common on the Internet now.

Task 3 Noticing language for certainty and caution

During their conversation, Chen and Guy show how certain they are about their claims.

3.1 Study the transcript of Chen and Guy's conversation on pages 226 and 227. Find the words and phrases they use to show certainty and caution (uncertainty). Write this language in the table below.

strong language to show certainty	cautious language to show uncertainty

3.2 Underline the words that show probability. How do they affect the certainty of each claim?

Task 4 Thinking critically about arguments

4.1 In Guy and Chen's conversation, which student presents his arguments in a strong way, and which one is more cautious or uncertain? Which way do you think is more academic?

4.2 What do Chen and Guy decide to do? How will this help to decide who wins the argument?

Guy and Chen look on the Internet and study the data they find together in order to decide whose argument it supports best.

Table 1 Main languages used on the Internet

languages	Internet users by language millions (2008)	world population for language millions (2008)	Internet penetration* by language %
English	464	1,247	37
Chinese	321	1,365	24
Spanish	131	408	32
Japanese	94	127	74
French	74	414	18
Portuguese	73	244	30
German	65	96	68
Arabic	41	291	14
Russian	38	140	27
Korean	37	70	52
World Total	1,596	6,710	24

* Internet penetration is the ratio between the number of Internet users speaking a language and the total number of speakers of that language.

Source: Miniwatts Marketing Group. (2008). Retrieved August 30, 2009, from http://www.internetworldstats.com/stats7.htm

Key words

world population
Internet penetration
world regions
stands for
gross domestic product (GDP)

Table 2 Internet users by region

world regions	Internet users millions (2008)	population by region millions (2008)	penetration* % of population	GDP** by region US$ millions (estimate)
Asia	657	3,781	17	16,774,002
Africa	54	975	6	1,518,911
Europe	393	804	49	18,394,115
South America	173	581	30	2,878,379
North America	251	338	74	17,080,000
Middle East	45	197	23	1,918,850
World Total	1,596	6,710	24	60,690,000

* Penetration is the ratio between the number of Internet users in a region and the total number of people in that region.

** GDP stands for gross domestic product. It is a measure of the wealth of a country.

Task 5 Preparing to listen

Work in pairs. Study the tables on page 170 and discuss what they show. Look carefully at the headings of the columns. Decide which data could be used to support Guy's or Chen's claims from Task 2. Use the questions below to help you.

Table 1

a Which language is dominant on the Internet now?

b Which languages might become dominant in future?

c Which languages already have a high percentage of their speakers with Internet access?

Table 2

d Which regions in the world have a large number of Internet users?

e Does the data suggest any reasons for these large numbers of Internet users?

f Which regions already have a high percentage of their population with Internet access?

g Which regions have the most potential to increase their Internet access?

Task 6 Listening

6.1 ⊙CD2-22 Listen to the next part of Chen and Guy's conversation. Find answers to the questions from Task 5.

6.2 Who wins the argument? What conclusions do the two students draw?

Task 7 Thinking critically about data

7.1 Listen to the conversation again. Read the transcript on pages 227 and 228 if you wish. According to Chen and Guy, how reliable is the data they have found? Decide whether the following statements about the data are True (T) or False (F). Write T or F in each box.

a The website explains how the data was calculated.

b The figure for the number of English speakers includes first- and second-language speakers.

c The number of first-language speakers of English is reported exactly.

d The Asian region probably includes China, India and South-East Asia.

e The figures for GDP give a precise value for the wealth of each region.

f Chen and Guy think that the data is reliable.

7.2 Is the data reliable enough to support the claims that Chen and Guy make in their argument?

7.3 How should Chen and Guy change their claims so that they could use this data as supporting evidence in an essay or project?

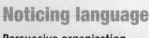

Noticing language

Persuasive organization

When Chen and Guy discuss the data, they can look at it and point to it, so they do not need to label the data exactly. They use the same moves that Roy Williams used in his proposal on page 159, but they use more simple language.

move	example
locating and labelling the data	*Look at Table 1.* *What about this figure: Internet penetration?*
claims about what the figures show	*A lot more Chinese go online now.* *We even got more speakers than English.*
descriptions of the data to support the claims	*We got 657 million Internet users in Asia, but that's only 17 per cent of the population.*
interpretation of the data: what it means, what conclusions can be drawn	*It shows which languages already have a high percentage of their speakers online.* *We got a lot of potential for increasing Internet access.*

Task 8 Thinking critically about interpretation

In their conversation, Guy and Chen interpret the data by drawing conclusions.

Where do they get the extra information which enables them to make these interpretations?

Task 9 Speaking

9.1 **Study the tables on page 170 again. Find out what the data shows about your region of the world.**

9.2 **Prepare to give a short talk about Internet access in your country and its potential to increase. Use your knowledge of your local region, as well as data from the tables, to support your claims.**

9.3 **Work in a group with other students whose countries are in the same region as yours. Compare your country's Internet access with theirs. Prepare a report comparing all the countries in your region to present to the class.**

Self study

Write a short report about the potential for Internet access to increase in your country and in your region. How does Internet access in your country compare with Internet access in your region? Use the data for Internet penetration and GDP on page 170 to predict how the use of the Internet might grow in your country. Bring your report to the next class.

Lesson 4
Language study

Guy thinks he might be able to use the data that he and Chen found on Internet use for a course he plans to take in semester 2. The course is about e-commerce, and one of the topics deals with new and emerging markets for selling goods and services on the Internet. Guy decides to write a report about the potential for increasing Internet access in developing regions.

Below are some tasks which Guy could use to write his report about the data. As you work on these tasks, compare your answers with the text you wrote for homework. This will help you to evaluate and improve your writing.

Task 1 Practising grammar patterns for labelling data

Below are some noun phrases that Guy could use to label the data in Tables 1 and 2 from Lesson 3, but the order of words is not correct.

Change the order of the words to make noun phrases that accurately label the data. Look at the headings for the rows and columns on page 170 to help you.

a speak who users English Internet

_____

b speakers number of the worldwide Chinese

_____

c the English of Internet speakers with proportion access

_____

d the Internet in number of Asia users

_____

e the North the population in size America of

_____

f the in the who African of people proportion have the Internet region access to

_____

Noticing grammar patterns

Comparing data and making claims

The data in Tables 1 and 2 is presented so that different groups of people – Internet users, language speakers, regional populations – can be compared.

Claims about the data can compare the relative size of the groups, or show which group is dominant.

pattern	claim
relative size *larger than* *smaller than*	*The number of Japanese speakers is larger than the number of Korean speakers.* *The GDP of the African region is smaller than the GDP of South America.*
dominance *largest* *smallest*	*The Asian region has the largest population.* *For the languages shown in the table, Korean has the smallest number of speakers.*

Descriptions of the data can be given to support the claims. These descriptions can also show relative size or dominance.

pattern	support for claims
relative size linking words signpost words	*127 million people speak Japanese, but only 70 million people speak Korean.* *The GDP of South America is about 2,878 billion US dollars. However, the African region has a GDP of only 1,519 billion US dollars.*
dominance maximizers minimizers	*Over 56 per cent of the world's population lives in the Asian region.* *Only about 1 per cent of the world's population speaks Korean.*

Table 1 Main languages used on the Internet

languages	Internet users by language millions (2008)	world population for language millions (2008)	Internet penetration* by language %
English	464	1,247	37
Chinese	321	1,365	24
Spanish	131	408	32
Japanese	94	127	74
French	74	414	18
Portuguese	73	244	30
German	65	96	68
Arabic	41	291	14
Russian	38	140	27
Korean	37	70	52
World Total	1,596	6,710	24

* Internet penetration is the ratio between the number of Internet users speaking a language and the total number of speakers of that language.

Source: Miniwatts Marketing Group. (2008). Retrieved August 30, 2009, from http://www.internetworldstats.com/stats7.htm

Table 2 Internet users by region

world regions	Internet users millions (2008)	population by region millions (2008)	penetration* % of population	GDP** by region US$ millions (estimate)
Asia	657	3,781	17	16,774,002
Africa	54	975	6	1,518,911
Europe	393	804	49	18,394,115
South America	173	581	30	2,878,379
North America	251	338	74	17,080,000
Middle East	45	197	23	1,918,850
World Total	1,596	6,710	24	60,690,000

* Penetration is the ratio between the number of Internet users in a region and the total number of people in that region.

** GDP stands for gross domestic product. It is a measure of the wealth of a country.

Task 2 Practising grammar patterns for data and claims

Look again at Tables 1 and 2 from Lesson 3, above and on page 174. Answer the questions below by writing sentences that make claims about the data. Use noun phrases 1–6 to label the data in your claims.

a Who forms the largest group online?

_____

b Which is larger worldwide, the number of Chinese speakers or the number of English speakers?

_____

c Who has the larger proportion of Internet access, Chinese speakers or English speakers?

_____

d Which region has the largest number of Internet users in the world?

_____

e How large is the North American population compared with the European population?

_____

f Which region has the least Internet access of all the world regions?

_____

1 Internet users who speak English
2 the number of Chinese speakers worldwide
3 the proportion of English speakers with Internet access
4 the number of Internet users in Asia
5 the size of the population in North America
6 the proportion of people in the African region who have access to the Internet

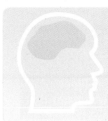
Task 3 Practising language patterns for supporting claims

Write some sentences to support the claims you made in Task 2. Make comparisons to show the relative size of the figures from Tables 1 and 2. To show the dominance of one language or one region over the others, you can calculate its proportion of the total. Use maximizers and minimizers to show your viewpoint.

Identifying correlations in data

In Table 2, the figures for the number of Internet users in a country and the GDP of a country seem to vary in similar ways. For example, Asia, Europe and North America are wealthy regions with a high GDP, and they also have high numbers of Internet users. When two sets of figures show a similar pattern of variation, this is called a *correlation*. However, this similarity does not mean there is a cause–effect link. When researchers observe a correlation, they conduct further studies to find out if there is any direct cause–effect relationship in the data. They report the correlation cautiously.

Task 4 Thinking critically about causes and effects

4.1 Look carefully at Table 2, on page 175, again. Compare the columns for the number of Internet users and GDP. The two sentences below suggest a cause–effect link between these two sets of figures. In each sentence, underline the cause and circle the effect.

   a The number of Internet users in a region determines the GDP of that region.

   b The GDP of a region determines the number of Internet users in that region.

4.2 Which sentence shows the more likely direction of a possible cause–effect relationship?

Task 5 Thinking critically about cautious language

The sentences above suggest a strong cause–effect link, rather than a correlation, between the GDP of a region and the number of Internet users. The ideas should be expressed more cautiously.

5.1 Tick 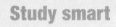 the best statement below to suggest a correlation.

a There is a link between the GDP of a region and the number of Internet users in that region. ☐

b When the GDP of a region increases, the number of Internet users also increases. ☐

c Regions which have a large GDP are also likely to have a large number of Internet users. ☐

d The GDP of a region is a factor in determining the number of Internet users in that region. ☐

5.2 Which sentence makes a claim that has no data in the table to justify it?

5.3 Change the other two sentences you did *not* tick so that they report the correlation more cautiously.

Study smart

Did you suggest a correlation in your text? Do you think there is a possible link between GDP and Internet access? Could the wealth of your country or region possibly be a factor that enables more people to go online? Suggest this correlation in your text, but be careful to use the correct order for the items in your sentence. Use language which shows that the correlation is not certain.

Noticing language patterns

Linking familiar and new ideas

Texts are easier for readers to understand if their sentences develop from familiar to new ideas. Sentence 1 below is easier for a reader to understand than sentence 2.

1. The number of Arabic speakers worldwide is around 41 million.

2. Around 41 million is the number of Arabic speakers worldwide.

For data in tables, the ideas that are familiar to a reader are in the titles and the headings of the rows and columns. When Guy and Chen searched for data on the Internet, they used key words. They then selected tables which included these familiar key words in their titles and headings. The new ideas are the numbers in the cells of the table.

Information can also be familiar to a reader if it has already been introduced earlier in the text.

Example:

Internet penetration for this language is <u>low</u>. The reason for <u>this low figure</u> might be …

In the first sentence above, *Internet penetration* is familiar – because it is a column heading – whereas *low* is new – because it reports the data. In the next sentence, both these ideas are now familiar, so they are put at the beginning of the sentence to prepare for further new information – *the reason*. The noun phrase *this low figure* labels the ideas as being familiar and creates a link back to the previous ideas.

Task 6 Identifying language patterns for familiar and new ideas

Below is a report on data selected from Tables 1 and 2 to show the potential for increasing Internet use in a particular language.

6.1 Study the tables on pages 174 and 175 in order to decide which language data is being reported in the text below. Write the same word in each gap.

(a) ☐ _____ has a much smaller population of speakers worldwide than English or Chinese. (b) ☐ The number of people who access the Internet in _____ is also much smaller. (c) ☐ _____ speakers account for only 414 million of the world population, compared with 1.25 billion for English and about 1.37 billion for Chinese. Only around 74 million people use _____ online. (d) ☐ However, Internet penetration for this language, at only 18 per cent, is much lower than expected. (e) ☐ The reason for this low figure might be because many _____ speakers live in the African region, which has some of the poorest countries in the world. (f) ☐ People in these countries probably cannot afford to buy computers, and their governments might not be able to maintain the expensive communications systems which are necessary to connect to the Internet. (g) ☐ Most people who use the _____ language on the Internet probably live in Europe, where Internet penetration has already reached almost 50 per cent. Therefore, it seems unlikely that Internet use in _____ will increase significantly.

6.2 Highlight familiar information at the beginning of each sentence above. Where has this information come from? Was it in a column heading (C), in a row heading (R), or in both column and row headings (C+R), or does it link (L) back to ideas that were introduced earlier in the text? In each box, write C, R, C+R or L.

Task 7 Thinking critically about familiar and new ideas

Look again at the text above. One sentence starts with new information. Which one is it? Why do you think it starts this way?

Study smart

Look at the beginnings of the sentences in your homework text. Identify familiar and new information. Do your sentences develop from familiar to new in order to help a reader? If not, make some changes.

Self study

Revise and redraft your report on the potential for Internet access to increase in your country and region. Bring your draft to the next class to exchange with another student. Use the checklist to evaluate your partner's new draft.

Evaluating data reports

The tasks in this lesson can be used to form a checklist for evaluating reports on data.

Content: Have you made general claims to highlight what the data shows?

Have you supported these claims with evidence from the data?

Have you interpreted the data based on correlations within it or your own knowledge?

Organization: Have you helped your reader by developing your ideas from familiar to new?

Language: Have you written noun phrases which accurately label the data?

Have you used language to show your viewpoint and how certain you are?

Lesson 5

Interpreting data differently

Aims

- to understand the claims in the debate about global warming
- to evaluate a website which assesses claims about global warming
- to assess specific claims about global warming using data

Maysoun has to prepare for a seminar on possible future changes to the climate caused by global warming. At postgraduate level, students are expected to research a topic so that they can discuss it in a seminar with their tutor and other students in order to reach a deeper understanding of the issues. Maysoun first consults an encyclopaedia to get a general overview before she considers the issues in more detail.

Key words

possible

future

a seminar

a deeper understanding

an encyclopaedia

overview

Discussion

- What do you know about global warming? What is the link between global warming and climate change? Is this issue controversial, i.e., do people have different viewpoints about it?

Task 1 Reading quickly for the main idea

Where in the text on page 180 can Maysoun find the types of information below? Write the correct paragraph number in each box.

a the link between global warming and climate change

b research methods to study global warming

c views of scientists who say global warming is not a problem

d a definition of global warming

e reasons for recent increases in the earth's temperature

f evidence that global warming is not a problem

Task 2 Reading carefully

Which claims below represent the views of most scientists (MS), and which ones are the views of the global warming sceptics (GWS)? Write MS or GWS in each box.

a 1 Recent global warming is mainly due to an increase in heat from the sun.

2 Recent global warming is mainly due to larger concentrations of carbon dioxide (CO_2) in the atmosphere.

b 1 Climate models are accurate, as they are tested against past measurements.

2 Climate models are inaccurate, as they do not consider all heat sources.

c 1 Increased concentrations of CO_2 are the result of increased temperatures.

2 Increased temperatures are the result of increased concentrations of CO_2.

Global warming

1. Global warming is an increase in the temperature of the land, seas and atmosphere of the earth. The sun provides most of the heat for the earth, but gases such as carbon dioxide and methane in the atmosphere absorb some reflected heat from the sun and stop it escaping back into space. This is known as the *greenhouse effect*. Carbon dioxide and methane are produced by animals when they breathe and by plants when they decompose, so there is a natural greenhouse effect which traps enough heat to warm the earth sufficiently for humans to live there. However, global temperatures have risen steadily over the past 150 years, with an increase in average surface temperature of about 0.74°C between 1905 and 2005. During this period, humans have burned much larger quantities of coal and oil, which released large amounts of carbon dioxide into the atmosphere. They have also cut down many forests, destroying plants which could absorb carbon dioxide as they grow. Thus, the main increase in greenhouse gas concentrations, which is thought to be responsible for the increase in temperature, is due to human activities.

2. Global warming disturbs the interaction between the oceans and the atmosphere, which regulates the climate and weather of the earth. It gives rise to long-term changes in climate. Scientists have studied this phenomenon with computer models of the climate. These models have to be simplified because of limitations in computer power and the complexity of the climate system. The models predict that the earth could be between 1.1 and 6.4°C hotter by the end of the 21st century, compared with 2000. Researchers test the accuracy of these models by running them from points in the past and comparing their predictions to actual past measurements of surface temperature. The models represent the past climate reasonably accurately. This gives confidence in their ability to predict the future climate.

3. A small group of scientists deny that global warming is a problem. These global warming sceptics claim that the main reason for global warming is not increased carbon dioxide in the atmosphere due to human activities, but increased heat from the sun. In addition, they suggest that computer models of the climate are inaccurate because they do not take into account the raised temperatures in urban areas due to human activity (known as the Urban Heat Island effect), which would increase the overall amount of warming that is observed. They also point to measurements of carbon dioxide and temperature from Antarctic ice cores which seem to show that, in the past, increases in carbon dioxide concentrations followed increases in temperature and were thus a result of warming and not the cause of it. The majority of scientists do not agree with these claims. However, many ordinary people find them attractive because if global warming is not a problem, they do not have to change their lifestyles.

Roadhouse encyclopaedia of environmental science. (2007) London: Roadhouse Publishers.

Task 3 Thinking critically about claims

How can Maysoun decide which of the claims from Task 2 are more likely to be true?

Maysoun finds a website, www.skepticalscience.com, which presents the sceptics' claims about global warming and attempts to challenge them. It uses data from scientific papers published in academic journals in order to examine the evidence for the claims of the sceptics. Before she refers to this website in her seminar, Maysoun needs to decide if it is a reliable source of information.

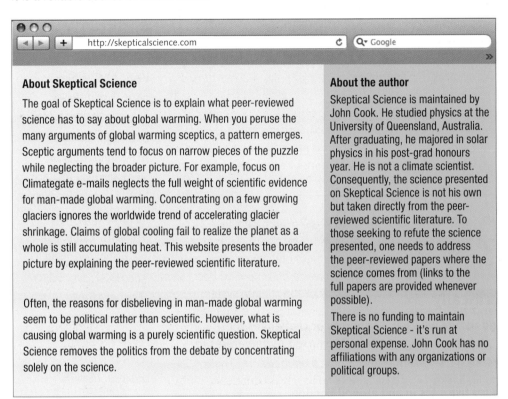

About Skeptical Science

The goal of Skeptical Science is to explain what peer-reviewed science has to say about global warming. When you peruse the many arguments of global warming sceptics, a pattern emerges. Sceptic arguments tend to focus on narrow pieces of the puzzle while neglecting the broader picture. For example, focus on Climategate e-mails neglects the full weight of scientific evidence for man-made global warming. Concentrating on a few growing glaciers ignores the worldwide trend of accelerating glacier shrinkage. Claims of global cooling fail to realize the planet as a whole is still accumulating heat. This website presents the broader picture by explaining the peer-reviewed scientific literature.

Often, the reasons for disbelieving in man-made global warming seem to be political rather than scientific. However, what is causing global warming is a purely scientific question. Skeptical Science removes the politics from the debate by concentrating solely on the science.

About the author

Skeptical Science is maintained by John Cook. He studied physics at the University of Queensland, Australia. After graduating, he majored in solar physics in his post-grad honours year. He is not a climate scientist. Consequently, the science presented on Skeptical Science is not his own but taken directly from the peer-reviewed scientific literature. To those seeking to refute the science presented, one needs to address the peer-reviewed papers where the science comes from (links to the full papers are provided whenever possible).

There is no funding to maintain Skeptical Science - it's run at personal expense. John Cook has no affiliations with any organizations or political groups.

Task 4 Thinking critically about sources

4.1 Find the website on the Internet or look at the text above. Use the checklist below, from Unit 4 Lesson 2, to evaluate the website. Find answers to the questions in the checklist.

Purpose: Why has the information been published?

Viewpoint: Does it show many different views?

Author: Is the author an expert in her/his subject?

Quality: Has the information been checked by other experts?

4.2 Is this website reliable? Should Maysoun refer to it in her seminar discussion?

Maysoun decides to examine some of the sceptics' claims using data from the website. The first graph on page 182 shows trends in the heat radiated from the sun (red line) and the average global temperature (blue line). The second graph shows trends in temperature at five locations in and around London. The brown line and the two blue lines show the trends at urban sites, while the two green lines show rural sites.

Task 5 Thinking critically about data

Study the graph below. Pay attention to what happens to the trends after 1975. Decide whether the graph supports or challenges the following claim made by global warming sceptics: *Recent global warming is mainly due to an increase in heat from the sun.*

Total solar radiance and global temperature 1885–2000

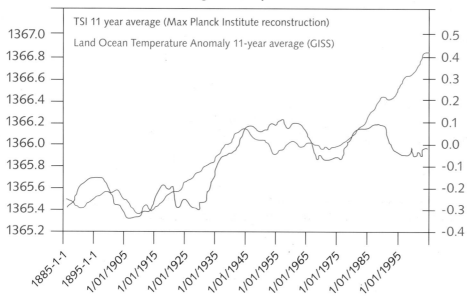

Task 6 Thinking critically

Study the graph below and decide whether it supports or challenges the following claim made by global warming sceptics: *The raised temperatures in urban areas affect the overall temperature trend.*

Temperature trends for five sites in and around London

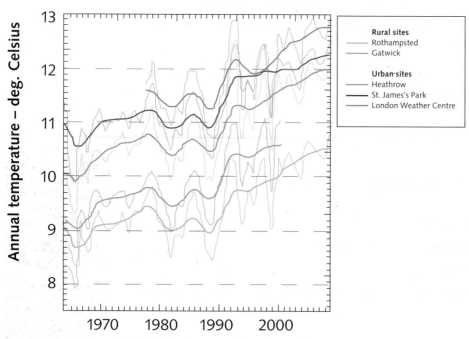

Jones, P. D., D. H. Lister, and Q. Li (2008), Urbanization effects in large-scale temperature records, with an emphasis on China, *Journal of Geophysical Research*, 113, D16122, 30 August 2008. Copyright 2010 American Geophysical Union.

Self study

Visit the web page http://www.skepticalscience.com/co2-lags-temperature.htm, and decide whether you accept the explanations given to challenge the following claim made by global warming sceptics: *Increased temperatures are not the result of increased concentrations of carbon dioxide.*

Try to find websites dedicated to scepticism about global warming, e.g., http://www.heartland.org/, and evaluate their claims. In particular, assess the evidence they provide to support their claims. Do they refer to data published in academic journals? Do they publish the data which supports their ideas so readers can assess it for themselves? Do you think their arguments are convincing?

Unit 10

Exams

Lesson 1

Revising

Aims

- to understand how to revise for exams
- to review the functional language introduced in this book
- to find and classify functional language in a text

It is near the end of the semester at Gateway University, and Maysoun, Chen and Guy are revising for their exams. They meet for lunch in the university canteen and discuss their revision strategies.

Study smart

1 What do you do in order to revise for exams? Discuss this with other students and make a list of activities.

In Unit 2 of this book, you read some guidance notes about studying smart, which means taking responsibility for your own learning. Students who study smart do three things.
- They are active: they do things for themselves.
- They are adventurous: they try new ways of learning.
- They are aware of how they learn: they think about how they complete tasks.

2 Which of the activities in your list can be described as *studying smart*? Can you give examples of how you are active, adventurous and aware of your learning?

Task 1 Listening

⊙CD2-23 Listen to the conversation between Maysoun, Chen and Guy, and answer the questions below.

a Who has the weakest exam strategy?

b Who is active and adventurous in her/his exam revision?

c Who is aware of how s/he learns?

d Are the ways of revising that the students discuss new for you? What advice could you try to follow?

Study smart

Maysoun had some good advice for Chen and Guy to help them improve their exam technique.

● Try to understand general concepts so you can apply them to specific examples.
● Look at previous exam papers to find out the kinds of questions that are asked.

This is good advice when preparing for an English exam, as well as for subject exams.

Task 2 Thinking critically

Look back to the book map on pages 4 and 5 of this book. Answer the questions below.

a Which column lists general concepts that classify language purposes? What are these general concepts called?

b These general concepts apply to many different subjects at university. Do you think they apply to your subject?

Task 3 Noticing functions

Study the sentences and complete the exercises below.

a Match each function a–h to an example sentence 1–8. Write the correct number in each box.

b Underline the language in each example which shows the function.

c Write another example sentence for each function which is related to your subject.

functions	examples
a describe purpose	**1** Keep windows and doors closed while you are working in the laboratory.
b describe position, shape, movement	**2** I chose to study Computer Science in order to use my mathematical skills.
c describe instructions, processes	**3** Chen feels happy because his current assignment is mostly programming.
d compare, contrast, evaluate	**4** The library at Gateway University is opposite the students' union.
e define, classify, give examples	**5** Gateway University used to be a technical college, but it became a university in the 1960s.
f explain change and development	**6** Almost one-half of Gateway University students come from outside the UK.
g explain cause and effect	**7** Information in the library is usually more reliable than information on the Internet.
h report and interpret data to show your viewpoint	**8** Pollution is a process which puts unwanted materials or energy into an environment.

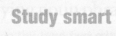
Task 4 Identifying key words

4.1 Underline words you do not know in the text below. Put them into two groups: technical vocabulary and general academic vocabulary.

4.2 Which words are explained in the text, e.g., using examples, synonyms or definitions? Which technical words only require an approximate understanding?

4.3 Look back to the language functions you identified in Task 3. Some words and phrases that relate to these functions are highlighted in the text below. Identify which function each colour relates to.

4.4 Find some more of the functions from Task 3 in the text below. Highlight each function with a different coloured highlighter pen.

Key words

poisoning
an illness
symptoms
vomiting
diarrhoea
stomach pain
public health
pre-prepared
diseases
campylobacter
contamination
raw
unpasteurized
dairy products
salmonella
come into contact with
death
are destroyed
the fridge

Food Poisoning

Food poisoning is a short-term illness which is caused by eating food that is contaminated by bacteria (the most common cause), viruses or poisons naturally present in fish or plants. It has a range of symptoms, which include vomiting, diarrhoea and stomach pain. The number of cases of food poisoning increased by about 10% every year in the 1990s. This trend has reduced recently, but it remains a concern for public health. The reason for the increase is thought to be due to a number of factors. People's habits changed in the 1980s. They shopped for food less frequently and stored food for longer. They bought food that was pre-prepared, but did not always cook it properly. In addition, increasing international travel enabled diseases to spread from other countries.

The most common cause of food poisoning is the bacterium campylobacter, which is found in raw or under-cooked meats, and unpasteurized dairy products such as milk and cheese. It takes only a small number of bacteria to make people ill. Another common cause is salmonella, which is transferred when raw foods including meat, dairy products and especially eggs come into contact with cooked foods. This bacterium is more dangerous than campylobacter because it can lead to more severe illness and even death. Both these bacteria are easily destroyed by proper cooking. Contamination often occurs because people do not wash their hands before preparing food or because raw and cooked food are prepared or stored in the same place.

In order to avoid food poisoning, it is important to follow some simple steps.
- Always wash hands thoroughly before preparing food.
- Keep kitchen work surfaces clean by washing them after each use in order to avoid contamination.
- Ensure food is cooked thoroughly before eating.
- Keep raw meat and fish covered and store at the bottom of the fridge.
- Rinse fruit and vegetables under running water before eating.

Adapted from: Parliamentary Office of Science and Technology. (2003). *Food Poisoning*. Postnote, 193. Retrieved February 12, 2010, from http://www.parliament.uk/post/pn193.pdf

campylobacter

Task 5 Thinking critically

In Task 5 of the Reading to Write exam, you had to link ideas in the text to your own knowledge and experience.

5.1 For each of the questions below, say what background knowledge you need to be able to answer the question.

    a How is buying Fairtrade products different from donating money to a charity such as Oxfam?

_____

    b Give two examples to show how members of a producer's family could benefit from being involved in the Fairtrade movement.

_____

    c What are the advantages of selling Fairtrade products in a supermarket compared with selling them in a Fairtrade shop?

_____

5.2 Look at the student answer to question c below. Say why it received no marks.

> In the 1970s, Fairtrade products were only available in Fairtrade shops and most consumers did not know about them. In the 1980s, the Fairtrade label was introduced so that Fairtrade coffee could be sold alongside ordinary coffee in shops and supermarkets.

Task 6 Taking notes

Through this course, you have practised taking notes in different formats. You used tables for comparison and contrast, classification diagrams, timelines to show development and cause–effect flow charts. These formats are designed to show the functional relationships between ideas.

In Task 6 of the Reading to Write exam, you were given a set of headings for your notes.

6.1 Look again at the note headings, below, and decide which function formed the main basis for the notes.

    Fairtrade [definition]

    Success [two ways to measure]

    Factors leading to success:

    1. fairness

    2. partnerships

    3. standards

    4. marketing

6.2 Look back to Tasks 4 and 5. Some questions relate to the headings in the notes above. Which questions could help you to take notes?

6.3 Use the checklist below to evaluate your notes from Task 6 of the Reading to Write exam. Compare with other students and with the model answer.

    • Are the notes mostly in note form?

    • Are the notes accurate, but not copied word for word from the text?

    • Are the notes relevant, with a definition, ways to measure success and factors leading to success?

Task 7 Writing

Below is a checklist similar to the one you used to evaluate an essay in Unit 8. The tasks below will help you to use this checklist to evaluate your writing.

Content   Did you:

- answer the question and follow the task instructions properly?
- include relevant and important information?
- understand what the reader needs, i.e., what is familiar and what is new – what needs to be explained and what does not?

Organization Did your paragraphs and sentences:

- maintain or develop topics clearly?
- move the reader from general to specific information?
- start with familiar information and then add new information?

Language   Did you:

- use your own words and not copy parts of the text?
- use suitable academic English?
- use a range of key words and language patterns for functions, e.g., defining and explaining reasons?
- label ideas accurately with noun phrases?
- link ideas in the text clearly using pronouns, repeated nouns and general nouns?

7.1 Content

Compare the model notes for exam Task 6 with your answer, and complete the exercises below.

a In your writing, can you find a definition of Fairtrade and the two ways to measure its success?

b Can you find some of the ideas listed in the model notes as factors which contributed to this success?

c Are there any parts of your essay which are not relevant to this question because you memorized them before the exam so you could include them in your answer? Cross these parts out, because they are not relevant.

d Are there any parts of your essay where you explain something your reader knows already? Cross these out, because your reader does not need this information.

7.2 Organization

The headings in the notes give you an overall organization for your writing. The model answer has five paragraphs.

Answer the questions below.

a Which headings in the notes match each of the paragraphs in the model answer?

b Does your answer have five paragraphs?

c Do you make it clear to a reader where one paragraph stops and the next one starts?

d Do your paragraphs develop from general to specific ideas?

e Underline the general idea at the start of each paragraph in the model answer. Can you find a general idea at the start of each of your paragraphs?

show general to specific paragraph development using noun phrases			
use some prepositional phrases, conjunctions, verbs and nouns for reasons and results			
use feedback to redraft texts			

Unit 9 I can ...	writing	speaking	comment
report data in tables and graphs			
make general claims about data			
support claims using data			
interpret trends and relationships in data			
identify familiar and new information in a table			
label data accurately using noun phrases			
show my viewpoint with appropriate caution			
think critically about interpretations of data			
evaluate writing using a checklist			

Unit 10 I can ...	writing	speaking	comment
revise effectively for an examination			
recognize functions in sentences and texts			
classify and record functional language			
analyze exam questions			
make notes from a text and use them to answer a question			
give a short talk and answer questions			
evaluate my performance in exams			
set new goals on the basis of my performance			

Additional material

Unit 4, Lesson 2, Task 3

Student A

features	items to be contrasted	
	information on the Internet	information in the library
purpose	to sell goods and services and ideas	
viewpoint		both advantages and disadvantages
viewpoint	only views which agree	
author		experts who have studied the subject deeply
quality	no one checks the quality	

Student B

features	items to be contrasted	
	information on the Internet	information in the library
purpose		to build knowledge and develop new ideas
viewpoint	mainly advantages	
viewpoint		views which both agree and disagree
author	anyone can publish anything	
quality		books and journals are checked by experts

Transcripts

Unit 1, Lesson 1, Task 1

CHEN: Hello, I'm Chen. I'm from China. I'm pleased to meet you.

GUY: Hi Chen. I'm Guy. Good to meet you, too. What are you studying?

CHEN: Computer Science, a BSc. But first I have to finish my English course. How about you?

GUY: I'm in my second year – BA in International Business. How long is your English course?

CHEN: Seven weeks.

GUY: So you already know your way around. I'm going to the supermarket. Want to come?

CHEN: Hello, Maysoun. Guy, this is my friend, Maysoun. We're both studying English.

GUY: Hi. Are you doing Computer Science too?

MAYSOUN: No, Environmental Studies. A master's. What about you?

GUY: A BA in International Business. I'm from here, I mean the UK, but I want to travel. Where are you from, Maysoun?

MAYSOUN: Syria. I'm here with my husband and son.

CHEN: Have you both got time for a coffee?

Unit 1, Lesson 1, Task 4

GUY: Why are you doing English? You both sound OK to me.

MAYSOUN: We're doing it to learn English for university studies, especially writing.

GUY: Good idea. Written coursework is difficult, even for me. This year I'll have to write much longer texts than I did at school – more than 2,000 words.

MAYSOUN: Yes, that's what I found in my BSc. But I think my master's will involve lots of reading, too.

CHEN: I don't think there's much writing in a Computer Science course.

GUY: Is that why you chose it?

CHEN: No, I'm studying Computer Science so that I can get a good job with a high salary. Why did you choose your degree subjects?

GUY: In order to get a job where I can travel and meet people. There'll be students from lots of different countries on my course this year.

MAYSOUN: I want to learn about environmental issues in developing countries.

Unit 2, Lesson 1, Task 1

STUDENT 1: Where's Engineering?

GUY: Civil or Electronic?

STUDENT 1: Electronic.

GUY: That's in Computing in the north of the campus, a three-storey building next to Chemistry, see, here.

STUDENT 2: What about Geology?

GUY: Between Petroleum Engineering and Environmental Science, in the east of the campus.

STUDENT 3: I'm looking for Management and Accounting.

GUY: They're both in the Business School. That's the large complex behind the library, on South Avenue.

STUDENT 4: Where can I find a computer to use?

GUY: There are open-access computer labs in most buildings. Look for these computer signs. I think the nearest one is in the library, just there on the right.

STUDENT 5: We need to see Professor Watson.

GUY: Which department?

STUDENT 6: Biology.

GUY: That's in the Environmental Science Building, on the top floor.

STUDENTS: The Amartya Sen Lecture Theatre? Alan Turing Laboratories? Hydrology Workshop?

GUY: Wait, wait! Sen is in the Business School, ground floor. Just walk through the library. Turing Labs are in Computer Science, but I'm not sure which floor. Hydrology is in the Civil Engineering Institute, that's on another site, not this campus. But there's a free shuttle bus from in front of the students' union, opposite the library – do you see the bus stop there?

Unit 2, Lesson 5, Task 4

CHEN: Hi, Guy. You look worried. Is something wrong?

GUY: Not really, I have to see my tutor, Dr Malik, this afternoon, that's all.

CHEN: Isn't he very friendly?

GUY: No, he's OK, but I didn't study very well last year and I know he's going to give me a hard time. He says I have to change.

CHEN: Why, what happened last year?

GUY: I failed my exams last May – had to do resits, that's why I'm back early.

CHEN: Resits?

GUY: Take my exams again. I was a bit lazy and I wasted time. I missed some lectures and I never went into the library because I thought I could find everything on the Internet. I didn't hand in drafts to my lecturers so I didn't get much feedback. I thought that if I just met the final

---

Key words

in
in the north of
a three-storey building
next to
between ... and
in the east of
the Business School
the complex
behind
the library
on South Avenue
there are
open-access
labs (laboratories)
signs
nearest
on the right
department
the top floor
lecture theatre
workshop
ground floor
through
institute
another site
a shuttle bus
there is
in front of
opposite

deadlines, I'd be OK. When I started to struggle with the work, I didn't want to tell anyone.

CHEN: But now you've passed your resits, right?

GUY: Yeah, but Dr Malik wants me to show him a study plan this afternoon and I don't know where to start.

CHEN: I read about how to study on the Computing website this morning. There's a list. And I've got some notes from my EAP class. Maybe I can show you?

GUY: Really? Thanks. Maybe I can use them. I want to do well this year – I don't want to waste another summer vacation studying for resits.

Unit 3, Lesson 2, Task 1

GUY: We're going to have beans on toast. It's cheap, and healthy if you use wholemeal bread and not that white stuff you keep buying!

CHEN: OK. I can make the toast, but I don't know how to make the beans.

GUY: You get them in cans, already prepared. It's easy. Here's a can. I'll tell you what to do, but you have to do everything – the same way you teach me how to do stuff on the computer.

First, open the can with a can opener and put the beans in a pan.

Right. Next, turn on the gas and heat the beans gently. Stir them with a spoon occasionally so that they don't burn at the bottom. No, not that one – it's dirty! This one's been washed! That's great.

Put two pieces of bread in the toaster and switch it on.

Heat the beans until they just begin to bubble.

CHEN: The beans look ready now.

GUY: Put the toast on plates and put the beans on top of the toast. Enjoy!

Unit 3, Lesson 3, Task 2

Part 1

PROFESSOR LEACH: Good morning, everyone. Welcome to the Rachel Carson Teaching Labs. I'm Professor Leach and I am your course leader for this module. Today, I'm going to talk to you about some of the key things you have to do to make the labs a safe working environment for all of us. Then I'll show you a short health and safety video. Finally, you will all learn how to grow bacteria colonies from a water sample taken this morning from our beautiful campus lake. Perhaps when we look at the results tomorrow, this will discourage you from drinking the water or eating the ducks!

Unit 3, Lesson 3, Task 4, Exercise 4.1

Part 2

PROFESSOR LEACH: First, I'll talk about the fire hazards. The university has to carry out a fire drill every year in every building on campus. It's the law. This is to practise leaving the building quickly and safely. So please make sure today that you know the correct fire escape route from this lab and the fire assembly points, where you have to meet outside. Always leave the building on hearing a continuous ringing of the fire alarm. Oh – yes, and the fire alarm has to be tested weekly. This is on Tuesday mornings at 9.15. It's a short ring, to show it's not a real fire or a drill.

We are in a science laboratory where there are a number of hazards, including fire. We have to minimize the risk from these hazards. So please, when using Bunsen burners:

1. Keep loose papers and folders well away from the flame.

2. Minimize the height of the flame by adjusting the gas tap.

3. Until you need to heat something, make sure the flame is visible by adjusting the air hole.

4. If you leave anything heating over a flame, check it frequently.

5. Remember to turn Bunsen burners off before leaving the lab.

No need to tell you to keep your hands out of the flame! But you should also keep your hands away from the hot tap – the water is very hot! And always protect your hands with heat-resistant gloves when holding anything containing hot liquid.

Any questions so far?

MAYSOUN: Yes, you mentioned fire escape routes. How do we find these?

PROFESSOR LEACH: Good question. See the green notice above the door, with the person running? You have to follow those signs. Find the route after the practical.

MAYSOUN: OK. Thank you.

Key words

the hazards
to carry out
a fire drill
the law
the fire escape route
continuous
the fire alarm
the fire assembly points
to minimize the risk
the flame
by adjusting
the gas tap
visible
the air hole
frequently
heat-resistant
liquid

Unit 3, Lesson 3, Task 4, Exercise 4.2

Part 3

PROFESSOR LEACH: Next, infection. Some of our practicals involve working with pathogens, i.e., with infectious material. There are many ways we minimize the risk of infection. It's good to see that you are all wearing your lab coats. That's the first point: always wear your lab coat in the labs to protect your clothes. Splashes on your clothes or skin are a source of infection.

Other points are:

1. Tie back your hair if it's long.

2. Cover any skin cuts with a waterproof dressing before you come into the lab.

Key words

pathogens
infectious
to protect
splashes
a source
tie back
cover
a waterproof dressing

3. When pipetting, minimize splashes by slow delivery.

4. Always clean spills using gloves and paper towels that have been soaked in disinfectant.

5. Keep doors and windows closed while you are working.

6. Wipe down surfaces after use.

7. Wash your hands before leaving the lab.

8. When you wash your hands, wash them thoroughly for at least a minute and keep the soapy water on your hands for at least 30 seconds.

We've also had accidents with centrifuges. Those machines at the back. Read the safety notice: "Ensure the lid is fully open before removing the contents".

Many accidents are trips and falls. Avoid these by keeping the floor clear of bags and coats – put them in the lockers. Keep safe by being aware of everything in your environment.

I'm going to show the video now, but first, are there any more questions?

ANGELA: Yes, you mentioned disinfectant. I can't see any here. Where is it kept?

PROFESSOR LEACH: Good point. It should be on every bench. We'll put some out in a minute.

PETER: You said we're going to experiment with some water samples. Do we have to write a report?

PROFESSOR LEACH: Yes, I'll explain all that after the health and safety video. Let's watch it now.

Key words
pipetting
delivery
spills
have been soaked
disinfectant
wipe down
surfaces
thoroughly
soapy
centrifuges
ensure
the lid
the contents
accidents
trips
falls
avoid
by keeping ... clear of
the lockers
by being aware of
bench
to experiment

Unit 3, Lesson 4, Task 2

DR CHARLES: Good morning, everyone. I'm Dr Charles and this is Lecture 1 in the Hydrology course. I hope you are all in the right place! Genetics 1 is in the next lecture theatre if anyone wants to move. Today, I'm going to talk about the water cycle, although we should refer to it by the technical term *hydrologic cycle*, that's H-Y-D-R-O-L-O-G-I-C.

First, I'll give a brief outline of the basic cycle to remind you about what I'm sure you already know from school. Then we'll start looking at the different stages in the cycle in much more detail, in particular at the roles played by geology and vegetation in the process.

There are three main stages in the hydrologic cycle. Let's start where most water – something over 90 per cent – is stored on the earth, the ocean. In the first stage, water is evaporated from the surface of the ocean by the heat of the sun and by air movement. The resulting water vapour is carried in the atmosphere, often visibly as clouds. When clouds reach land, in particular hills, the water condenses and falls as rain. This stage is known as precipitation, that's P-R-E-C-I-P-I-T-A-T-I-O-N. In the final stage, *runoff*, that's the two words *run* and *off* together as one word, some of the water runs from the land back into the ocean through river networks. But what happens to the rest of the water?

Key words
hydrology
genetics
technical
hydrologic
a brief outline
basic
in detail
the roles played by
geology
vegetation
stages
the earth
the ocean
vapour
the atmosphere
condenses
precipitation
runoff

Unit 3, Lesson 4, Task 3

DR QUINN: The P.I.E. cycle is a process for continually improving plans in an organization such as a business. The three steps are shown in this flow diagram.

In the first stage, planning, the improvement objectives are specified, together with the actions needed to achieve them. These action plans are then implemented in the organization. After a suitable period of time, the plans are evaluated by comparing the results of the implementation with the original objectives. This analysis leads to the specification of the next set of objectives and action plans, which brings us back to the beginning of the cycle.

Unit 3, Lesson 5, Task 2

Part 1

DR BELL: The waterfall model describes a process where software development goes down these five steps. You have them on your handout. Water always flows downhill, and this process is called *the waterfall model* to show that it moves in one direction (see these arrows), like a waterfall. It's not easy going back to an earlier step to change things. It's also very expensive. So the emphasis is on getting things right at each step, in particular the first step.

Unit 3, Lesson 5, Task 3

Part 2

DR BELL: In the first stage, the requirements for the system are gathered by talking to the customer and other people who will use it. These requirements are analyzed very carefully and in great detail. Requirements analysis is probably the longest stage in the process. This is to make sure the requirements are fully understood before the system is designed.

In the second stage, the system is designed. This means that the customer requirements are converted into software requirements by describing what the software will do. This involves dividing the system into its component parts so that they can be developed simultaneously by different teams. The design stage specifies what the programmers have to achieve.

Next, the code (the computer program) is written. In other words, the functional description of the system is converted into instructions that computers can follow. This is called the implementation stage, and is often the shortest in the process. At this stage, each programmer's purpose is to make the program efficient, adaptable and bug-free.

Verification is the next stage. The whole system is installed and tested and evaluated to ensure that it does what it should do and that it's acceptable to users, for example, by checking compatibility with other systems that the customer uses. It has to meet the requirements identified in the first stage.

Finally, once the customer has taken delivery, there is the maintenance

Key words

continually
plans
steps
stage
objectives
specified
implemented
evaluated
original
the analysis
leads to

Key words

the waterfall model
development
steps
downhill
in one direction
the emphasis
in particular

Key words

the requirements
in detail
are gathered
the customer
are fully understood
can be designed
are converted
describing
dividing
component parts
simultaneously
the programmers
the code
functional
the program
efficient
adaptable

stage. At this stage, the system may need to be changed slightly. There is usually an agreement with the customer to maintain or take care of the system for the time it's in use, for example, by solving problems that arise or renewing parts of the system that can be improved.

Unit 4, Lesson 1, Task 1

MAYSOUN: Have you got some ideas about what you want to write?

CHEN: Not really. I searched for computer-based learning on the Internet and I found some information on Wikipedia. That's all I've done so far.

GUY: I used the Internet for my assignments last year, but my lecturers told me to find more reliable information.

MAYSOUN: Yes, Wikipedia is a good place to go for an overview, but they want to see if you know how to use other sources to find information.

GUY: My lecturers also said I should have my own ideas and compare them to the information I find.

MAYSOUN: OK, so let's think what we all know about learning on computers and learning in classrooms. Chen, what did you find on Wikipedia?

CHEN: Well, they say it's more convenient using computers. You can study any time and you can take more time if you need to.

GUY: That's true, but you have to know how to study smart with computers; you have to set your own deadlines, because there's no teacher to set them for you and remind you about them. I think I would never finish my course if it was all computer-based learning.

CHEN: Well, it can be cheaper, too. You can study at home, so you don't need to travel and live in another country.

MAYSOUN: Yes, it's more flexible. You can study at home and work at the same time. I had to give up a good job to come here. My husband gave up his job, too.

GUY: I like classrooms because you can discuss ideas with other students and the teacher. Computers are less sociable.

Maysoun: I like classrooms better, too. I like to see people when I talk to them.

CHEN: We had lots of discussions on the pre-sessional course, but I didn't like class discussion because I can't speak quickly. I like discussing on the computer – I have more time to think what to say.

Unit 4, Lesson 2, Task 2

Part 1

LIBRARIAN: Welcome to Gateway University library. My name's Marie Macdonald. Today, I'm going to give you a general introduction to the library so that you can learn to use it effectively and efficiently.

In order to use the library effectively, you have to be able to find reliable

Key words

bug-free
verification
is installed
acceptable
compatibility
to meet the requirements
identified
maintenance
an agreement
in use
renewing

Key words

searched
on the Internet
Wikipedia
assignments
reliable
sources
compare
convenient
to set deadlines
flexible
to give up
sociable

Key words

introduction

information from many different sources. You also have to know that the information is relevant for your purpose. In order to use the library efficiently, you have to be able to find relevant and reliable information quickly so that you do not waste your time. I'm going to cover two main aspects today.

- I'll start by contrasting the different sources of information and explain how you can decide which ones are more reliable.
- Then I'll explain how we organize the books and journals in the library so you can find them easily.

Part 2

LIBRARIAN: OK, so let's think about sources of information. If you want to find information, what do you usually do?

STUDENT: Look on the Internet.

LIBRARIAN: Yes, that's what most people do; they search on the Internet. Probably you use one of the search engines such as Google or Yahoo, but is that the best way to find information for your degree subject? Let's think about some of the differences between information on the Internet and in the library. This will help to decide if the information is reliable.

First, we can think about purpose: why is the information put on the Internet or in the library? Well, people often put information on the Internet so they can sell you things, whereas we keep information in the library so students and lecturers can build their knowledge about a subject and develop new ideas. There are many web pages to sell goods and services, but there are also others to sell ideas.

Then we can consider the viewpoint of the information. When people want to sell ideas, they only show the advantages of the ideas and not the disadvantages. They show the views of people who agree with the ideas and not views that disagree. In the library, we try to keep a wide range of information, which includes many views about the advantages and the disadvantages of the ideas.

Another important difference between the Internet and the library is the author. Anyone can publish their ideas on the Internet. However, published books and journals are usually written by experts, people who have studied the subject deeply for a long time. These sources have been checked by other experts, such as editors, to make sure that they are reliable, in other words, that their quality is good. No one checks the quality of most information on the Internet. Now it is true that there is some good-quality, reliable information on the Internet, but you have to learn how to recognize good quality.

So, to summarize what I've said, you can decide if information is reliable by thinking about its purpose: Why has it been published? Is it trying to sell ideas? Then you can think about the viewpoint: Does it show many different views? Or does it show just one view? You can find out if the author is an expert in his or her subject. Has he or she published a lot of other books? Finally, you can decide if the information has been checked by other experts. This is a good checklist to evaluate reliability.

I hope I've convinced you that the library is a good place to find information. So now I'll move on to explain how we organize the books and journals.

Key words

relevant
contrasting
journals

Key words

the search engines
whereas
build knowledge
develop
goods and services
consider
the viewpoint
the views
agree
disagree
a wide range
includes
the author
publish
however
experts
deeply
have been checked
editors
it is true that ... but
to recognize
to summarize
finally
a checklist
to evaluate
reliability
convinced
move on

Unit 5, Lesson 1, Task 5

DR CHARLES: Today, I'm going to talk about the water cycle, although we should refer to it by the technical name 'hydrologic cycle', that's H-Y-D-R-O-L-O-G-I-C.

First, I'll give a brief outline of the basic cycle to remind you about what I'm sure you already know from school. Then we'll start looking at the different stages in the cycle in much more detail, in particular at the roles played by geology and vegetation in the process.

There are three main stages in the hydrologic cycle. Let's start where most water – something over 90 per cent – is stored on the earth, the ocean. In the first stage, water is evaporated from the surface of the ocean by the heat of the sun and by air movement. The resulting water vapour is carried in the atmosphere, often visibly as clouds. When clouds reach land, in particular hills, the water condenses and falls as rain. This stage is known as precipitation, that's P-R-E-C-I-P-I-T-A-T-I-O-N. In the final stage, *runoff*, that's the two words *run* and *off* together as one word, some of the water runs from the land back into the ocean through river networks.

Unit 5, Lesson 1, Task 6

Next, the code (the computer program) is written. In other words, the functional description of the system is converted into instructions that computers can follow. This is called the implementation stage, and is often the shortest in the process. At this stage, each programmer's purpose is to make the program efficient, adaptable and bug-free.

Unit 5, Lesson 5, Task 1

GUY: Hello, you two! How's it going?

CHEN: Not bad, not bad. But too much work!

MAYSOUN: Me too. So many new ideas and new words to learn.

GUY: Don't your lecturers explain them?

MAYSOUN: Yes, mostly, but so quickly! And I have to remember them all.

CHEN: Sometimes I think I know a word, so I don't pay enough attention in a lecture, and then I find out it means something special in computing and I feel a bit lost.

GUY: Give us an example.

CHEN: Fields and gates. I know about gates; old Chinese cities have gates. This university's called Gate-way. But in computing, logic gates are electronic. They control what a computer does with information. And fields are nothing to do with farmers.

MAYSOUN: Yes, I thought a sink was in the kitchen where I wash the dishes! But in ecology, a sink is somewhere that something's stored, like heat or carbon. There are so many new technical words in my courses. I've started a different vocab notebook for every module. One for

> **Key words**
>
> logic gates
> control
> a sink
> carbon

hydrology, one for ecology and one for microbiology.

CHEN: That's cool! My vocab notebook's a mess. It's nearly full and I can't find the words I want. But with different books for different modules, there's more space and you've got some basic organization. I think I should write mine again, in separate books. How do you organize each book? I mean, by topic or what?

MAYSOUN: Alphabet. Each book has four pages for each letter of the alphabet. It's enough for now, but some pages are filling up fast.

CHEN: I think I'll start a new book for each module, like you. But I'll still write the words in the order I find them, a new page for each day. If I want to find words, I can usually remember when I wrote them. But maybe this is just a waste of time – I've got another assignment to prepare!

GUY: No! If you do it – I mean reorganize them, it'll be good. It's – like – a good way to revise them. But why not write on cards? Then you can change the way you organize the words any time you want.

CHEN: I see: flexibility. Even better! I can set up a database. Then I don't need to buy notebooks or cards. This is great!

GUY: Have you got a dictionary about computing to help you? I got a business dictionary last year and it was great for checking technical terms. The bookshop's got some new specialist dictionaries. We could go and have a look.

CHEN: Hey! Before we go, can I ask a favour? I have to give a presentation soon. Can I practise with you both later this week?

MAYSOUN: Fine. Is Thursday evening OK? I work late on Thursdays.

CHEN: Yes, sure. But where can we go? I've got to do PowerPoint.

GUY: I'll ask Dr Malik if I can use a Management seminar room. I'll tell him I need to practise presentation skills with some other students.

CHEN: Good thinking, Guy!

Key words

ecology
microbiology
a mess
alphabet
cards
a database
specialist dictionaries
ask a favour
a presentation
work late
good thinking

Unit 5, Lesson 5, Task 5

LIBRARIAN: Now, let's think about how you can find information in the library. What subjects are you studying?

MAYSOUN: The environment.

LIBRARIAN: OK, can you be a bit more specific?

MAYSOUN: Water in the environment?

LIBRARIAN: OK, that's a good topic. So how could you find information in the library about this topic – water in the environment? Well, our library uses the Dewey Decimal system. Dewey was the name of the man who invented this system, and it's a decimal system, which means it's based on decimal numbers. Each book or journal in our library has a number, and the books are stored on the library shelves in order of those numbers. So you just need to know the number of the book you want to read and you can find it.

The Dewey Decimal system has ten very general categories such as

Key words

the Dewey Decimal system
was invented
are stored
in order

Social Science, Science or Technology. Then each of these general categories is divided into ten more specific topics. For example, in Social Science we have Economics, and in Science we have Mathematics, Physics or Earth Sciences. Each topic has a number, for example, Social Science is 300 and Economics is 330. Science is 500 and Earth Sciences is 550.

These topics are divided again so they are even more specific. More specific topics have longer numbers. So within Earth Sciences, at number 551, we can find Hydrology – the study of water. However, we can also find information about water if we look under Technology and Applied Sciences at number 600. We can find Engineering at 620 and Water Engineering at 627, or Waste Water Engineering at 628. We can add a decimal point and more numbers to make the topics more specific, so at 628.16, we find the environmental effects of waste water.

Of course, there are many books even on this specific topic, so the system uses letters as well as numbers to distinguish different books. After the number, we have the first three letters from the surname of the author. For example, a book written by one of our lecturers, Dr Susan Charles, about the environmental effects of waste water, has a Dewey Decimal number 628.16 CHA.

Unit 6, Lesson 1, Task 1

GUY: This is my mum and dad at their graduation. They met here when they were undergraduates in the 80s. I think my family has been involved with Gateway for quite a long time. This is my dad's father. He was here too, in the 60s. It used to be a technical college then, but it became a university while he was studying, so he got a degree and not just a diploma. His family were working class and he was the first person ever to have a degree. They were so proud. Actually, I think some members of my family studied at Gateway soon after it was set up. It started as a college where working-class people could better themselves, you know, learn how to read and write properly. That was around 1860, I think.

Unit 6, Lesson 1, Task 2

GEORGE BLACKSTONE: Thanks for coming along. My name is George Blackstone and I live here in Summerford. I was at Gateway University in the 1950s; of course, it wasn't called Gateway then but, erm, I'll come to that later. I studied Engineering when I was at university – but now – well, I'm retired, of course, as you can see and, erm, I'm interested in local history. So today I'm going to talk to you about the history, erm, the history of the university, and I'll tell you about some of the important events that have happened in its lifetime.

Gateway University is really quite young when you compare it to universities like Oxford and Cambridge. They were founded in the 12th century, whereas Gateway started only about 150 years ago, in 1864. However, it has seen a lot of changes in its lifetime. It was started by two local businessmen. They were concerned because, erm, because there were no

Key words

Social Science
Economics
Earth Sciences
a number
Applied Sciences
Engineering
waste water
a decimal point
to distinguish

Key words

graduation
in the 80s
has been involved with
a technical college
a diploma
working class
proud
actually
was set up
started as
better themselves
around 1860

Key words

retired
to talk to you about
tell you about
have happened
were founded
years ago
has seen changes
in its lifetime
was started

schools for working-class people. They wanted a school – this is what they said – 'for the education of mechanics and engineers so they could have some practical understanding of science to apply to their work'. It wasn't a university then, of course, only a college. It used to award diplomas, but not degrees. It was called the Stevenson Institute – you know – after the famous engineer who invented the first steam locomotive.

The university was ahead of its time in terms of equal opportunities. Women began to attend classes in 1870, long before other institutions. This was mainly the result of a vigorous campaign by Jenny Ellis – erm – she was the wife of one of the founders but, erm, she was also a member of the Women's Movement. She convinced her husband that newly educated working men would want educated wives to talk to at home.

The Stevenson Institute quickly became very popular and, by 1880, the original buildings were overcrowded and in need of repair. The founders decided not to repair the buildings, but – erm – instead they decided to construct new buildings in the city centre. However, there were a lot of delays and the work was very expensive. So – erm – as a result, the institute experienced some financial problems – erm – so bad, in fact, it nearly had to close. Fortunately, it was rescued by a wealthy inventor who owed his fortune to his early studies there – at the institute. So, of course, the institute wanted to thank him for his support, erm, and they decided to change the name to include his name, so that's when it became the Morgan-Stevenson College.

Now, the college expanded throughout the 20th century and, in particular, it developed a reputation in the fields of Science and Engineering. It was given university status in 1967 – so this meant that it could award degrees. At the same time, a decision was made to relocate to a purpose-built campus outside the city – this campus that we are on now. It used to be a large estate, but the buildings were demolished long ago. The only thing left is, erm, part of the original arched gateway at the entrance. It was decided to rename the college *Gateway University*, to mark the move to the new campus. A new logo was designed and, erm, as you know, it features the gateway. So the university I went to in the 1950s had a different name and was located in a different place.

Since the 1960s, the main expansion has been in the number of international students who attend the university. Now, I think, more than one-third of the students on campus come from overseas, and there is also a large range of distance-learning programmes for students to study in their own countries.

So, I hope that's given you an idea of some of the changes in the history of the university, but if you have any questions …

Unit 6, Lesson 2, Task 9

MAYSOUN: My lecturers keep using a word, *revolution*; what do they mean?

GUY: Well, a revolution is usually a time when there are big changes in politics, you know, a new government, like the French Revolution. Is it like that?

Key words

mechanics
engineers
called ... after
steam locomotive
ahead of its time
equal opportunities
long before
a vigorous campaign
the Women's Movement
popular
original
overcrowded
in need of repair
instead
to construct
experienced
financial problems
fortunately
was rescued
wealthy
owed his fortune to
expanded
developed a reputation
university status
award degrees
to relocate
a purpose-built campus
estate
were demolished
arched
the entrance
to rename
to mark the move
a logo
features

CHEN: No, it's not politics. My lecturers talk about the Information Revolution. It's a huge change in technology. Because, you know, 30 years ago we didn't have PCs or mobile phones or the Internet. What would life be like without these things now? Terrible!

GUY: Oh, OK, you probably mean the Industrial Revolution in the 19th century.

MAYSOUN: Yes, that's one they talk about. Climate change started with the Industrial Revolution. What was the Industrial Revolution?

GUY: It's like Chen says, a big change in technology. In the 1840s, steam engines were the new technology. They made industries more productive – it changed the way people worked – but they used a lot of coal, which caused pollution.

MAYSOUN: I think I see. The Industrial Revolution was a big change but it was bad for the environment. Now we have to convert to renewable energy, which is good for the environment. It's another big change.

CHEN: Yes, maybe it's called the Green Revolution? Green for the environment.

MAYSOUN: No, actually I know about the Green Revolution. That was in the 1960s, when they started using tractors and fertilizer and pesticides to grow cereals. You can increase farm production, but it uses a lot more energy, too. It was like the Industrial Revolution, but in the countryside, not in the factories.

Key words

revolution
politics
government
industrial
climate change
steam engines
coal
renewable energy
tractors
fertilizer
pesticides
cereals

Unit 6, Lesson 4, Task 2

JENIFER: So, Guy, let's look at your writing. What are you unhappy about?

GUY: Well, I put some ideas from my textbook in my introduction, but I'm not sure I did this in the right way.

JENIFER: Well, let's talk about the easy things first. Did you show in your text which parts you borrowed? Do you know how to do that?

GUY: Not really. I think I have to give a reference.

JENIFER: Yes, that's right. You need a short reference in the text – we call that an in-text reference – to show your reader the part you borrowed – and you also need a full reference at the end of your essay so that your reader can find and read the same textbook. So for your textbook, the short reference would be …?

GUY: Dyson, 2008?

JENIFER: Good, that's right, and you need to put that in brackets to separate it from the other parts of your text. Now, what about the full reference for the end? Remember, your reader has to be able to find the book – so what information do they need?

GUY: The author and the date, erm, and the title of the book, too, I guess.

JENIFER: Yes, that's right, but they need the author's full name – the family name first, and then the initials – and they also need the publisher and the place where the book was published.

Key words

unhappy about
to give a reference
a short reference
an in-text reference
a full reference
the publisher

Unit 6, Lesson 4, Task 3

JENIFER: OK, let's look now at what you wrote. How did you decide which ideas to borrow?

GUY: Well, I thought I should start the essay with a definition. And then I thought I could talk about the history of the co-operative movement, so I borrowed some parts from my textbook about the history.

JENIFER: The parts you borrowed from the textbook – did you change them?

GUY: Not really. I joined some of the sentences together and I changed a few words. I didn't need to change much. The book said everything in a good way, so I just used the words in the book.

JENIFER: Do you think that's what your lecturer wants – J.R. Dyson's words from his book? Does that tell your lecturer what *you* know, or what J.R. Dyson knows?

GUY: Well, erm – you mean the lecturer wants J.R. Dyson's ideas but my words.

JENIFER: That's right. If you can put his ideas in your words, then you show that you understand them.

GUY: I see – but, erm, it was OK at secondary school, erm, I mean to copy and paste information from the Internet for projects. I did that in my first year at university, too, and it seemed to be OK. Most of the lecturers didn't say anything.

Jenifer: Did you get good grades in your first year?

GUY: No, well – actually – I didn't and, erm, one of my lecturers said I should find better-quality sources in the library.

JENIFER: OK, so maybe what you did is not a good way to borrow ideas – at least at university. Let's see if we can find a better way. The way you wrote your introduction is called *knowledge telling* – that's when you tell everything you know about a topic. That's what you did about the co-operative movement. That's usually how students write at high school, because it shows that they know facts. But at university, you need to do *knowledge transforming* – that's when you transform – or change – the way the ideas are written to make them fit your writing purpose.

GUY: So how do I know what my writing purpose is?

JENIFER: You can find your purpose in your essay question. Look at your question. It doesn't say *What is the co-operative movement and how did it develop?* But that's the question you answered. Your essay question really says *Why did the co-operative movement decline?* The way the question is written tells you that your readers already know what the co-operative movement is. You only need to give a very brief summary in your introduction to tell them the topic.

GUY: So how do I do that?

Unit 6, Lesson 5, Task 3

CHEN: Hi, Maysoun. We just wanted to get your opinion about my

---

Key words

joined ... together
to copy and paste
at least
knowledge telling
knowledge transforming
transform

that feedback on exams should involve putting the answers online, so students can compare them with what they wrote.

Unit 7, Lesson 3, Task 2

CHEN: The term malware comes from two words, *malicious*, meaning *bad*, and *software* – which I'm sure you all know means *computer programs*. Malware is a kind of software that is written deliberately to damage a computer system or to use it without the knowledge of its operators. Malware is hostile in that it never benefits the infected system or the owners and it may cause considerable damage to the organization.

There are many different kinds of malware. They are classified on the basis of how the hostile code first enters and then operates inside the computer. I am going to tell you about three main types of malware: viruses, worms and Trojan horses.

A computer virus is a computer program that can reproduce itself just like a biological virus and can copy itself into, or infect, different computer files in the system. It can infect the memory or the files, for example JPEG images and Word documents. It is transferred from one computer to another over a computer network or inside a moveable device such as a USB drive or CD. In the 80s and early 90s, viruses could be very destructive. They carry a set of instructions (called a *payload*) which can do anything a normal user can do. Deleting data from a hard disk was a favourite. Of course, like biological viruses, killing your host quickly is not a good idea, so some only activated themselves on a certain date or just hung around, using up resources. People used to write them just to see how far they would spread.

Viruses can be further divided into resident or non-resident viruses depending on their behaviour. Non-resident viruses look for other files to infect and infect them. Resident viruses stay resident in the computer's memory and infect files as the operating system loads them.

A worm is a malicious computer program that doesn't need human activity to transfer it, but can spread from host to host without users doing anything. Some worms carry a payload of hostile code, for example designed to delete files, send out malicious e-mails or even untraceable spam. A worm can do all of these things without the system operator's knowledge.

A Trojan horse is a program that appears to be useful, but in fact hides hostile code within it. Because it looks attractive, people may not think about the danger inside it. For example, you may see a funny screensaver offered for free on the Internet and download it. While the screensaver is running it may be copying your files, allowing someone else to see them or even to control your computer.

Unit 7, Lesson 3, Task 3

GUY: Wow, I didn't get much of that. That's very technical. I switched off after 30 seconds.

Key words

malware
malicious
meaning
deliberately
operators
infected
hostile
kinds
operates
viruses
worms
Trojan horses
reproduce
computer files
JPEG images
Word documents
moveable
a USB drive
CD
destructive
a payload
deleting data
a hard disk
host
activated
hung around
using up
resources
resident
non-resident
behaviour
operating system
human activity
untraceable spam
appears to be
screensaver
download

CHEN: Is it too boring?

GUY: No, No. Er ... I'm just not good with computer stuff. Maybe you should slow down a bit.

MAYSOUN: But the slides are good: very clear. They help to understand some of your points. I think the main problem is how you speak.

GUY: Yes, you need to look at us – so you know from our faces if we can understand.

MAYSOUN: And you should say 'good evening' or something and tell us your name and topic. Chen, you seemed to be reading the whole presentation.

CHEN: Yes, I know I have to memorize it, but I couldn't manage that.

MAYSOUN: That's the problem! If you read, your mind is thinking just about reading. It isn't thinking about explaining. Your words come out very flat and there's no emphasis in your voice.

CHEN: I don't know how to do that. My speaking is so bad.

GUY: No! Not true! You always explain stuff very clearly to me when you help me with my computer.

MAYSOUN: Why don't you put your text away and just explain it from the slides?

Unit 7, Lesson 3, Task 4

CHEN: Right, hello. Good evening. My name's Chen Zhiqiang, and I'm going to talk about malware. First, Er ... what is it? Er ... it's some code that gets into a computer system but you don't know. It's hidden. And it's never good; sometimes it's dangerous. So do you ... have you ever had a problem with a virus? That's malware.

OK. There are three main kinds of malware: viruses, worms and Trojan horses, but they are different. Viruses came first in computer history. They can copy themselves inside the computer, but only .... but first they need to get into the system. That's usually by an infected USB drive, etc. Viruses can carry some bad code, for example to delete your hard drive. There are two types of virus, and it depends on what they do. One kind, resident viruses, live in the memory and infect files when they are loaded but ... er ... non-resident viruses go looking for files to infect.

The next one, worms, are more clever. They don't need ... er, they can get from one computer to another by themselves. They can send e-mails or spam from the system and the ... er ... person, the operator knows nothing about what's going on.

Finally, a Trojan horse is really bad. It usually looks useful, but has hostile code. People download it because they don't know what's in it. Here, an example was a free screensaver but when people downloaded it, it was able to do things without those people, operators ... they didn't know. A Trojan horse can even let someone else see what you're doing, or can control your computer.

I enjoyed that. OK, I see what you mean. More interesting, but it's not very academic! And I forgot some stuff.

MAYSOUN: Yes, but everybody does the first time. You just need more practice.

CHEN: How much practice?

MAYSOUN: Many times. On your own; in front of the mirror; with different friends.

GUY: Why not record yourself?

CHEN: You're right! That will help me to notice if I forget some stuff.

Unit 7, Lesson 3, Noticing language patterns

'malicious   malicious

ope'rator   operator

danger, endanger, dangerous

infect, infected, infection

pollute, pollution, pollutants, polluter

operate, operator, operation

malware, malicious

flexible, flexibility

memorize, memorization

specific, specifically, economic, democratic

ability, responsibility

organization, international

identify, specify, verify

special, social, financial

malicious, delicious

Unit 7, Lesson 4, Task 3

MAYSOUN: My lecturers keep using a word, *revolution*; what do they mean?

GUY: Well, a revolution is usually a time when there are big changes in politics, you know, a new government, like the French Revolution. Is it like that?

CHEN: No, it's not politics. My lecturers talk about the Information Revolution. It's a huge change in technology. Because, you know, 30 years ago we didn't have PCs or mobile phones or the Internet. What would life be like without these things now? Terrible!

GUY: Oh, OK, you probably mean the Industrial Revolution in the 19th century.

MAYSOUN: Yes, that's one they talk about. Climate change started with the Industrial Revolution. What was the Industrial Revolution?

GUY: It's like Chen says, a big change in technology. In the 1840s, steam engines were the new technology. They made industries more productive – it changed the way people worked – but they used a lot of coal, which caused pollution.

MAYSOUN: I think I see. The Industrial Revolution was a big change but it was bad for the environment. Now we have to convert to renewable energy, which is good for the environment. It's another big change.

CHEN: Yes, maybe it's called the Green Revolution? Green for the environment.

MAYSOUN: No, actually I know about the Green Revolution. That was in the 1960s, when they started using tractors and fertilizer and pesticides to grow cereals. You can increase farm production, but it uses a lot more energy, too. It was like the Industrial Revolution, but in the countryside, not in the factories.

Unit 7, Lesson 5, Task 2

NICK: OK, everybody, erm, let's get started. So, erm, I'd like to introduce Chen. Chen studied with us on the pre-sessional course last summer and, erm, now he's in the first year of his Computer Science degree here at Gateway. He's agreed to come along today to give you an idea about university life – thanks for coming, Chen.

OTHERS: Yes. Right. Thanks!

NICK: So, Chen, what would you say is the biggest challenge for an international student, erm, like yourself, to study in the UK?

CHEN: Well, erm, hi, everybody.

OTHERS: Hi, Chen

CHEN: Do you like your classes with Mr Nick?

OTHERS: Yes, sure, we do.

CHEN: He's a good teacher – taught me a lot. But, you know, right now I face my biggest challenge.

NICK: Really, what is it?

CHEN: Well, I have to prepare a presentation, erm, you know, a talk for one class, and then we have to … have to discuss, you know, discuss about the topic. And, you know, Chinese students, we are not always easy to do it.

OTHERS: Mmm, yeah.

CHEN: I see a lot of Chinese students here – maybe you've got some ideas about that.

CHEN: See what I mean? Come on, somebody, speak!

XIAOHUA: We … we don't like speak out. Teacher … erm, teacher in middle school she told us, 'You should spend time to listen, not discuss.'

Key words

middle school

MONICA: Mmm, Chinese teachers like students to be quiet. If you speak, you will get into trouble. Chinese saying 'Trouble comes out of your mouth.'

MIMI: Yes. Same in Thailand – in school, I mean. Mmm … don't be loud.

NICK: So you think that, erm, it's the way you learn at school? That's why you don't want to speak?

CHEN: Yes, erm, I think it's part of that. So, in class the teacher has the most power, you know, to control everything. And we feel a great distance between the teacher and the student. So, I think we will speak if we have permission, you know … if the teacher looks at us and says our name.

XIAOHUA: But also … erm, we come to class, you know, because we lack of knowledge, so we want to hear what the teacher say instead of the opinion from other student.

OTHERS: Mmm, yes.

XIAOHUA: So, we, erm, we hide our opinion – not hide – but when we are young, we have to see ourself as in the group, so we don't want to waste time for the group if we express our personal opinion in a class.

MONICA: Mmm … it is traditional culture … erm, the Chinese traditional culture emphasizes our harmony very much. Harmony is the basic rule, to rule the whole society and just like harmony tries to avoid challenge and … argument. You know, that is why many Chinese students don't ask questions and, erm, don't disagreement to others.

AMIR: But … erm, I think not only Chinese. In Iran, it's the same. You can ask questions after the class, but you cannot interrupt the teacher. The teacher is in control.

XIAOHUA: Amir, you are not like us: you are happy to answer quickly; ask any question you want. Are all students in Iran like you?

AMIR: I am not so confident, Xiaohua. I'm afraid to be judged in public. So I'm also afraid to lose my face.

NICK: Right. I've heard that before: *lose face*. What does it mean?

OTHERS: It's a big thing; very important.

AMIR: Erm … like, respect; what others think of us; our social value.

MIMI: Mmm. Have to think about it all the time and be careful for others. Mmm. Don't embarrass others.

MONICA: Yes, mmm. If you don't know others … I think … erm, we don't like speaking with strangers. We need time to get familiar with people to express our ideas.

NICK: Alexei. You're very quiet today! What do you think? Do you have this kind of feeling in Russian culture?

ALEXEI: Actually, well, being afraid to speak in front of strangers, no. …. as you know, I speak a lot, all the time. But that's because you guys don't speak! Actually, Nick, you usually have to tell me: be quiet, Alexei! But we do have this idea of *face,* and people definitely don't want to seem stupid. Maybe it's not so strong as for you guys.

CHEN: I think another thing is … is when it is only your opinion, erm … like it is not an important topic and we won't need to think about it a lot, then we can contribute. But … erm, you know, for an important discussion … unless we are really sure what we want to say, I think we will keep silent.

AMIR: Yes, I think that too. In Iran, when there is discussion you can describe your mind exactly, but in UK … er, in English you cannot describe what's in your mind, so you don't want to say anything.

XIAOHUA: It's true. The language is a big problem. Chinese students need time to think about it and … erm, sometimes we are afraid to make mistakes, you know, worried to be stupid. In an important discussion, erm, I need a lot of time to think about the questions and prepare using a dictionary.

NICK: But I think, erm … everyone needs to prepare for a formal discussion. I mean, I would definitely not feel comfortable either if I had to do it without preparation.

CHEN: Actually, I had a good experience. My friend Guy … erm, he suggested me to attend the international students' meeting, you know, and, erm, we went together. I was really nervous … erm, didn't want to speak but, erm … the other students on the committee were, you know, like really friendly. And there was one student from Thailand. She made lots of mistakes but, the others … well … erm, they didn't care about that because she was the secretary and she … erm, she wrote the minutes, you know, and that's a really difficult job. I got a lot of confidence seeing how they supported her.

OTHERS: Really! Yeah!

NICK: So it sounds like joining the international students' meeting was a good way for you to gain confidence.

CHEN: Yes, really it was. And you can join, too. My friend Guy was right. He said it's important to contribute. If you stay silent, then people think you're not interested. Or they think you are stupid. So, even though you feel afraid, you must contribute.

NICK: Well, I think that's maybe all we have time for now. Chen, thanks a lot for coming along. I think that's been really useful for the class to hear.

OTHERS: Yeah, sure. It has.

NICK: The message seems to be: you have to contribute. Don't worry about your language or what others think about you.

Unit 8, Lesson 2, Task 2

DR CHARLES: Hi, everyone. I hope you've packed everything on the list – boots, water bottles, etc.? Before we go, we should … er, … I guess this is the first field trip for some of you, so you might be wondering what these forms are for? Just standard procedure. It's university policy for everyone to be well prepared, er … so there are no accidents or unnecessary risks in the field. In fact, when you're working in the field

Key words

feel comfortable

Key words

packed
might be wondering
standard procedure
university policy

professionally, you always have to complete a risk assessment like this before you even start – and I mean *always*.

A hazard is anything that may cause harm – like a fire. Risk is a combination of the probability of a hazard – how *likely* you are to be harmed – and the severity or seriousness of a hazard, how *badly* you may be harmed. Well, fortunately, not too many hazards for us this weekend. We're not rock climbing or tree climbing, so serious falls are unlikely. But we are following water courses, small streams, so some of you will probably have minor trips, slips and falls. Just be very careful near the water and make sure you always work in twos or threes so you can help each other. John here is a first aider and has the first aid kit for the cuts and scratches that most of you will get. It's November and you may get a little wet and cold, so bring extra warm clothes in your bag each day we're out.

Everyone should have in their equipment pack a fluorescent jacket. Wear it at all times outside – not just so I can find you, but to make you visible to car drivers when we walk on the road ... er ... to prevent accidents. I know it's ... it may not seem very exciting or adventurous, but, believe me, the most likely serious accident for an environmentalist in the field is a road traffic accident going to or from the site. A low probability, but serious if it happens. Any questions?

MAYSOUN: What about poisonous snakes and spiders?

DR CHARLES: No, that's a good question. Er ... we don't have any really dangerous wild animals in the UK – so a bite is unlikely. There's really no risk for us, because we're not attempting to catch any animals at all. However, you will definitely, all of you, get bitten by insects, so take some insect repellent and cover as much skin as possible ... to reduce itchy bites. There's one in particular, not an insect, but a tick. It's not common where we're going, but it can give you a serious disease called Lyme disease. It's possible ... unlikely, but serious if you get it. So cover up and use the insect cream to repel any ticks. If you find a tick on your skin, tell John immediately and he'll deal with it. No need for sun cream in November, by the way. Oh! I can see you're expecting to have fun, but there's serious work to do! Let's fill in these forms, and then we can go.

Unit 8, Lesson 4, Task 1

XIAOHUA: I just don't understand Martin – what he wrote on my essay.

CHEN: OK, I think I do. But first, is this the question: *The greenhouse effect*? It's just a topic. We need more detail, because that's a big topic. What *about* the greenhouse effect? What specific things does the assignment say you have to write?

XIAOHUA: What do you mean? I think I have to write everything I know.

CHEN: Not really. Not at university – it's not so simple. Usually, for a big topic like this, you have something specific to write about. I mean: *What are the causes / the effects?* or *Describe the process* or *What are the problems?* or *How can they be solved?* Does he want you to write about different countries – say, compare China and the USA?

XIAOHUA: Not sure! I lost the paper he gave us. I think I have to say something about 'my country'.

CHEN: Let's check on the Foundation Year website ... yes, here it is, see, International Issues, Assignment 2. *Write a 500-word essay to explain to one of your classmates the link between the Industrial Revolution, global climate change and developing economies. Include what you know about your country.* See, that's more specific. But it doesn't say anything about the greenhouse effect.

XIAOHUA: It's too difficult. I can't write 500 words. I don't know about Industrial Revolution or economy in my country, just only computing.

CHEN: Yes. You've done a kind of high-school English essay – not academic. Don't worry, I used to write like this when I first came here. We can make it more academic. And I know a bit about the Industrial Revolution, from Guy and Maysoun.

Unit 8, Lesson 4, Task 2

CHEN: Nick – our EAP teacher – he gave us some handouts last summer. Here, this one is about feedback on writing – to show us exactly what he was thinking when he marked our essays. Let's look at that first.

XIAOHUA: Wow, There's so much.

CHEN: Yes, but it's not bad when you break it down, kind of analyze it. There are only three categories. See, first, Content: that's about your ideas. And it's what we've been talking about, doing exactly what the instructions say you have to do – the topic and the specific things. And he wants to see key information, not just all your ideas on the topic. Also, you have to think about who'll read it.

XIAOHUA: I see, I think I understand that bit: follow instructions, get good ideas, think of reader.

CHEN: Exactly! Next, Organization. That's about linking ideas. When you start a paragraph, give general information first, then add more and more specific information about it. And each paragraph is about something different. But for sentences ... er ... you have to use some familiar information first in a sentence, then add new stuff.

XIAOHUA: I never done that before. Just I done topic sentence.

CHEN: Yes, like that ... but a bit more. I'll show you. And language, that's ...

XIAOHUA: I know, grammar, and mine is so bad!

CHEN: It's a kind of grammar ... er, but it's academic ... first, well, you kind of link, er ... summarize new information to start a new sentence ... you use words like *this* or *this problem*. It's hard to explain, but I can show you. Also, your essay is all about what causes things, and, er .... what things are results – just what Martin says. We made a page of grammar patterns with Nick about that. Here it is: Cause and effect language. Let's draw a flow diagram for each paragraph to get the ideas clear first, then we can use the grammar patterns to link the ideas in sentences.

Unit 8, Lesson 5, Task 3

DR MALIK: Guy, I really like this. This is so much better than your other stuff. You've really thought about this. I like your explanation of how the co-op's principles are helping it to become more competitive again.

GUY: Really? I was a bit worried that I was off topic.

DR MALIK: No, it's really interesting, but I'll say more about that in a bit – perhaps you could expand your last paragraph, maybe more examples. And write more about different ethical concerns.

GUY: How do you mean – examples of ...?

DR MALIK: Well, just go round a co-op store and note some of the goods on sale that are examples of fair trade, environmental standards, and so on – read the labels. Can you do that?

GUY: Oh yes! I work there some nights, stacking shelves for the next morning's business.

DR MALIK: Great. But look at the competitors as well. Because they're getting into ethical trading, too.

GUY: Like a mini survey?

DR MALIK: Exactly. The services are important, as well: insurance, banking, travel agencies. They've got big ethical concerns. Check them out. There should be plenty of information for customers online.

Oh, don't forget ... what sources did you use? You need to put them in your essay; there's only one here at the moment.

GUY: Yes, of course, I'll do that. I got a couple of books from the library, but they were published in the 90s. They explained about the co-op principles and about the competition from big supermarket companies. But I wanted to know about now, today ... erm, to be honest, I was a bit worried by the title I chose from your list – you know, about the decline – because, as I got into it, I realized that the decline isn't the whole story. I know that the Summerford co-op is doing very well. I talked to the manager; he's doing an MBA. He knows a lot about ethical trading. He gave me some more up-to-date journal references.

DR MALIK: Well, so you didn't like my title? Haha! Good, I like to see a bit of critical thinking in my students. Maybe we can change the title. You're right, it's getting a bit out of date. How about: *What factors contributed to the decline of the co-operative movement in the UK in the 20th century, and will it survive in the 21st?*

Guy, you're heading for an A on this assignment if you can develop the ideas at the end. You might think about this area, I mean co-operatives and ethical trading, for your honours dissertation[1].

Unit 9, Lesson 3, Task 2

GUY: It's obvious, Chen, the main language on the Internet is English. Everyone knows that. English is the global language. It's everywhere. Look at pop music and films and sport ...

CHEN: ... Uh huh, and science and technology and business. I know,

Key words

off topic
environmental standards
stacking shelves
getting into
mini
travel agencies
check them out
doing very well
as I got into it
the whole story
up to date
out of date
How about?
heading for
honours dissertation

Guy, but just because it's a global language, that doesn't mean it's the main language on the Internet.

GUY: Mm. OK, but the Internet was started by an American and used for scientific research at the beginning so – you know – for a long time English was the only language. It's probably still the dominant one.

CHEN: That's true but, erm … I think other languages are maybe catching up now. Chinese, for example. A few years ago, no one could access the Internet in my country, but now lots of people can.

GUY: OK, but maybe they use English when they go online.

CHEN: Yeah, well, they used to, but – you know – there are lots more websites in Chinese now. I think most people in China probably use Chinese on the web – and remember, we got a lot of people – about 1.5 billion.

GUY: Sure, but there are lots of people who speak English, too – like me, for instance. It's my first language, but there are places like India where it's an official language, and lots of people like you learn it as a foreign language.

CHEN: How many, do you think?

GUY: I don't know, but we can find out. Let's Google it.

Unit 9, Lesson 3, Task 6

GUY: Well, this is a surprise for me. Look at Table 1. In fact, I was right. There are more people who access the Internet in English than the other languages but, erm, Chinese is really close now.

CHEN: Uh huh.

GUY: I'm sure that at one time, more people used English than all the other languages together, but it looks like that's no longer true.

CHEN: Yes, erm … it's like I said – a lot more Chinese go online now and, erm, we even got more speakers than English. Actually, I didn't know that before. But maybe this table includes Chinese speakers in all parts of the world, not just China.

GUY: Mmm … I don't know, because I'm not sure how they calculate the numbers, especially for English.

CHEN: No.

GUY: The website gives the … some sources for the data, so I followed the link, but they don't show the calculations either. It says they just count one language … you know … for each person, but how do they know which language?

CHEN: I don't think … I don't think, erm, they know accurately. They just … you know … estimate.

GUY: Yeah, probably.

CHEN: I saw one website that said, erm, the number of English speakers is between 275 and 450 million, but that's a lot less than this table shows. … erm, maybe they mean only first-language speakers.

[1] This is an extended piece of research, done in the final (senior) year of a degree course and sometimes called the *honours project*.

GUY: Probably. I saw another web page – it was about the future of English and, erm, it said English has 375 million first language speakers, but there are around 750 million people learning it as a foreign language, like you.[2]

CHEN: Wow … so many! What about this figure: *Internet penetration*?

GUY: Well, I think it shows which languages already have a high percentage of their speakers online. So you can see Japan is high, and Germany and Korea have quite high percentages, too.

CHEN: Oh, OK – I know for Japan and Korea that's probably because most of the speakers are just in one small country … erm … not spread around the world.

GUY: Same for Germany, too. It's a big country, but its share of the world population is small.

CHEN: Look at Table 2. Where is China? In Asia?

GUY: Uh huh.

CHEN: But we don't have that many people.

GUY: I think they put India in with China and call it Asia. Probably it includes South-East Asia, too. It's like the UK is in with Europe and Canada is together with the USA in North America. So it's not really very accurate data, either.

CHEN: OK, so we got 657 million Internet users in Asia, but that's only 17 per cent of the population so, you know, we got a lot of potential for increasing Internet access.

GUY: Yes, and it's a wealthy region. Look at the figure for GDP – it's a bit less than North America and Europe, so more people are getting rich and can afford to access the Internet.

CHEN: That's right.

GUY: Probably the online population will grow quickly.

CHEN: Not like North America and even Europe; most of the people in these regions already have access, so these figures won't change much in the future – even though they're rich, too.

GUY: So, Chen, I guess we both win. I was right about English. It's still the most popular language on the Internet, but you were right about Chinese, probably it will soon grow bigger than English – so I'd better get going with my Chinese lessons!

Key words

not very accurate

Unit 10, Lesson 1, Task 1

MAYSOUN: Hello, you two. Good to see you. Are you busy these days?

CHEN: Me, yes. I'm revising for my exams.

GUY: Mmm, me too.

CHEN: Actually, I'm really worried, 'cos, you know, I haven't done exams like this before. I mean, only exams in high school. So I don't, erm, I don't know what I have to do.

MAYSOUN: Well, we did English exams on our pre-sessional course –

Key words

these days

[2]Figures sourced from: http://www.britishcouncil.org/learning-elt-future.pdf

don't you remember? – and we got a practice exam to try first. Can you find some practice exams for your subjects?

CHEN: Hey, good idea. The lecturers said they would put the answers for our exams up on the intranet, you know, after the grades are published. Perhaps they leave them up there from last year. Should be the questions, too. I can check.

GUY: But, you know you, won't get the same questions. I'm sure they change them every year.

CHEN: Maybe … but I want to see what kind of questions they ask … check if they ask us to write some code, you know, like a program. I know I can do that … in fact, I'm good at doing it and, you know, it means I don't have to write lots of English. So … maybe I can work on … erm, try to get good marks for that part.

GUY: Mmm, I see, yes. I haven't looked at past exam papers before, but it might work for me too. Probably Dr Malik sets the same kind of exam question each year for International Marketing. Usually, I just read through my textbooks until I get bored and then hope that I'll remember enough to answer the questions. Mmmm. It doesn't sound very systematic, does it?

MAYSOUN: No, it doesn't! If you can predict what kinds of questions you're going to get, you can spend more time studying those parts of the subject. Then you don't waste your time.

GUY: Yeah, I know I need to improve my exam technique. I don't want to do resits again this year, like I did last year. But revision is always a problem for me. You both seem so organized. What else do you do to revise, Maysoun?

MAYSOUN: Well, at postgrad level, we have to show that we understand general concepts … erm, you know, general ideas, and we can apply them to specific cases or situations. So, when I revise, I pick out the general concepts and, erm, I summarize them very briefly, erm … I make very brief notes … and then I think about how these concepts applied to the case studies we discussed in class. And I try to find another example, maybe in a book and, erm, do the same thing, you know, apply the same concepts to that example. So then, when I go over my brief notes, I can remember the concepts but I can also remember how I applied them.

GUY: Wow! That's fantastic. I think that would work for my International Marketing course – we had lots of case studies to discuss. They were the most interesting part of the course. I'm going to try that this afternoon.

Key words

good at doing
past exam papers
sets the question
systematic
It doesn't … does it?
No, it doesn't.
what else …?
pick out